ENDO

As the pages are turned in "The Chick in Charge", you will find yourself engulfed in a journey that postured Mary Parker to be a very successful and "Take Charge" leader. This book is a testimonial to her walk of faith, courage, wisdom, strength, and understanding of the importance in transferring knowledge to other generations. Here within is the fearlessness in the entrepreneur's love for God and how being faithful over a little demonstrates that you can be trusted with much.

Blair Underwood
Hollywood Actor & Director

When I think of Mary Parker, I first and foremost think of the word "persistence." In both her personal life and professional life, she has been "persistently" strategic, focused, and courageous. She does not shy away from "tough" decisions, and she always takes the best and highest road.

Ingrid Saunders Jones
National Chair, National Council of Negro Women (NCNW)
Senior Vice President, The Coca Cola Company

I met Mary Parker midway in my career. She is awesome. She is a star, absolutely a star, among all the great people I've worked with. It was never a doubt in my mind that she had a great future at GM or that she would have a great future wherever she chose to work and to participate. I'm not surprised at where she is today, and I believe her best days are ahead of her yet.

Roy Roberts
Retired Vice President, General Motors

One whose life has been filled with challenges and triumphs—my beloved sister, Mary Parker. I write this endorsement with much pride and love for her. One who has tenacity, skill, love, humility, love for God and others, she has been on a journey of self-actualization and The Chick in Charge discovery for many years. Transparency is evident. May you be influenced by this reading and experience the power of God as He has directed Mary's life from a child in rural Mississippi to the CEO of a multi-million dollar enterprise.

Bobbie A. Powell
Executive Administrative Assistant to The CEO, ALL(n)1

Mary Parker's meteoric rise to the top of the business world is legendary. In this classic book, she gives explicit instructions and encouragement, based on her own experiences, in overcoming patriarchy, sexism, and race in the marketplace. "The Chick in Charge" will help to revolutionize and galvanize powerful women who are ready to soar to unimaginable heights. This is a must read.

Dr. E. Dewey Smith, Jr. Pastor/Teacher The House of Hope Atlanta

Mary Parker is a woman of strong convictions and integrity, and she knows how to get the job done. The Chick in Charge reveals her greatest attribute—selflessness. This book depicts yet another threshold in giving of yourself to benefit others.

John Eaves
Chairman, Fulton County Board of Commission

Watching Mary Parker build her business as one of the only women in a heavily male-dominated field has been intriguing. Her growth was observable, largely through the growth of her reputation and her persona, as opposed to the usual physical evidences of affluence.

Mary Parker has plotted a clear path to success by always taking the moral high ground. The more she has achieved, the more she has given. She recognizes her giving not just as an obligation, but more so as the privilege to serve which it truly is. These are the characteristics that make her such a very powerful role model.

The Mary Parker story is a seminal one. Its moral positioning is one that is more reachable and believable than those of great heroes of sport, entertainment, business, and politics.

Carlton E. Brown, Ed.D

To: Tina Rembert
Love is what Love does! May your journey be filled with all your dreams

My New Friend —

THE CHICK

in

CHARGE *5/4/19*

Life Lessons, Business Principles, &
Inspirational Tools for Optimum Success

Blessings & Love,

MARY H. PARKER

Mary P

With foreword by
Xernona Clayton
Civil Rights Advocate & Creator of The Trumpet Awards

MARKONE PUBLISHING

ATLANTA

THE CHICK IN CHARGE

Published by MarkOne Publishing
3645 Marketplace Blvd, Suite 130-370
Atlanta, Georgia 30344
A subsidiary of KDR Consulting, LLC

ISBN: 978-0-9972334-0-7

Library of Congress Cataloging-in-Publication Data:
An application to register this book for Cataloging has been submitted to the Library of Congress. Printed in the USA and Canada.

Sharon Frame, Former CNN Anchor/Writer
Executive Speaking Coach, Speaker

Mary Parker Bio head shot by Monica Morgan, International Photojournalist

Cover and book design by KDR Consulting, LLC ®
www.kdrconsults.com

Interior book design by A Reader's Perspective
www.aReadersPerspective.net

THE CHICK
in
CHARGE

Life Lessons, Business Principles, &
Inspirational Tools for Optimum Success

DEDICATION

Grandma, so many memories of our times together were revisited while writing this book. I realize that you were the original "Chick in Charge" and my inspiration in all I do. I was blessed to receive your mantle of strength, loving and sharing with others, entrepreneurial visions, and so much more. It's with that spirit, while writing this book, that I feel as though I'm having a conversation with you in heaven. I dedicate this book to you, as a manifestation of all you shared with me. I am because you were! Oh, by the way, your other grandchildren still tease me because I always called you "MY grand-mother", as though I had exclusive rights to you.

ACKNOWLEDGEMENTS

So many family members have sown into my life. And part of my success is the fruit of their labor. At the top of my list of acknowledgement is my loving mother Lorethia Robinson. There would be no Mary Parker or *The Chick in Charge* without her. She planted seeds early in my life by example. I watched her persevere and beat the odds as a struggling Mississippi sharecropper. Her determination to ensure a better life for her children helped to mold my strong character. Mother, I am thankful.

Then there was my "Golden Wonder" Godmother, Katie Daniels. She stepped into my life during a dry and depressing season. It was my Katie who pruned and watered me back to health. She then dared me to excel to heights in business I would never have reached without her wise counsel.

Like my Katie, Uncle Homer and Aunt Mae have transitioned to glory with God. But their added value to my life will never die. Both provided shelter, support and a shoulder to cry on when life got tough. Both were also there to celebrate my many career successes.

Success for me also comes from the bursts of sunshine that my daughter Chana and granddaughters, Amber, Essence and Jada bring to my life. I am so very privileged to love and be love by them. They light up my life with great delight and affection.

So do my seven siblings. They too have provided much love and support over the years. We have always been there for each other, no matter what. I can't think of a better caliber of people to be linked to by blood.

I am forever grateful to my immediate and extended family members who have truly been the wind beneath my wind.

FOREWORD

When Mary Parker was born, she brought great joy to the Robinson family. And although I was not there, my imagination leads me to believe that she entered this world with a broad, disarming smile on her face. She probably had a strong, determined look that declared, *World, I am here and I plan to occupy my rightful space.*

Being female was good enough for Mary's family. She was loved, nurtured and thoroughly cared for. She was clothed in a blanket of security and self-confidence, and given every right and opportunity to meet her life goals. However, society presented the antithesis of this charge. The broader world said women could not be seen in such an "apple-of-our-eye" vision. The female sector of society was not guaranteed equal rights. And there was another problem to face—Mary was not only a female; she was a Black female, which added another obstacle in historical context. However, time and determination proved the facts! The fact is that Mary succeeded against all odds!!! She excelled in her educational pursuits and proved, in every step of her journey, that she was prepared to face the world with all of its obstacles. She possessed a tough minded faith combined with a tender-hearted spirit.

Mary learned along the way that "life becomes what we make of it." What we make of life depends entirely upon how we manage the ideas in our head. We can actually achieve the impossible! The enthusiasm that comes from God-inspired faith gives one peak performance power.

It is easy to understand Mary's successes. She took charge early in life, set goals, chartered a course, believed she would succeed, and based her ultimate success on the character of God. He never fails! God can do great things through people who are dedicated to Him. Faith gives you the power to maneuver your way around the obstacles and dangers of life.

I will go before you and make
the crooked places straight.
~ Isaiah 45:2

You might not be able to remove obstacles nor tunnel through the mountain that lay before you, but no matter how steep the path might be, it can still be conquered if you work your way *around* the obstacles. Mary would not allow unequal treatment of women nor the injustice heaped on African Americans to thwart her efforts to excel and succeed. The good news is, eventually you do succeed! The crooked places become straight, and the mountain top is reached.

This *Chick in Charge* kept spiraling her way upward the mountain. She did not fail! Her drive, determination, positive mental attitude, strength of character, and respect for others have all attributed to her great successes. And so has her unflinching trust in God's promises.

Mary Parker is one of the most generous persons who ever lived. She readily shares her success with others and assists them to meet their goals. She deserves a gold medal for encouraging the discouraged. It is no wonder we find this chick sitting at the door. She was destined to be there.

Read the entire book to better understand her climb to success!

Xernona Clayton
Civil Rights Advocate
Creator, Trumpet Awards

CONTENTS

INTRODUCTION

THE CHICK IN CHARGE CHRONICLES MY LIFE'S JOURNEY FROM A share-cropping farm in rural Mississippi to serving as CEO of my own multi-million dollar security company.

Many people fail to succeed in life because they refuse to take charge! They waffle, waste time, and miss opportunities. Like Deborah, Ancient Israel's fourth judge, *The Chick in Charge* knows her worth and creates her own path to destiny.

The Biblical account of Deborah's life is documented in the Old Testament book of Judges. It suggests she was deeply respected as a female leader in a fiercely male-dominated society. Her military general once refused to go to war unless she went with him, even though it meant he would be disgraced. On this day, Deborah agreed but not without a word of caution to Barak, her Army Commander.

"Of course I'll go with you. But understand that with an attitude like that there'll be no glory in it for you. GOD will use a woman's hand to take care of Sisera," our opponent.

Deborah was a keen military strategist as well as a prophetess. She judged with great wisdom and godly insight, and people came from all over to seek her counsel and to settle their legal or domestic disputes. She rose to power at a time in history when women were not considered equal with men, much less regarded as political leaders. I can just imagine looking at her sitting at ease in a seat of power with a glory cloud of self-confidence hovering overhead. If given the opportunity to be teleported some four thousand years back in time to sit at her feet, I'd ask one question.

"So Judge Deborah, what makes you so comfortable in your calling?"

She would probably nod with a charming smile and respond, "Well, my friend, I am not in charge to make history nor to make a name for myself. God put me in charge to make a difference. And that brings me great comfort."

So here we have it. Just as Judge Deborah exemplified, making a difference is the true mark of a *Chick in Charge*. Making a difference in life means stepping up to the plate. It means showing up for duty and getting things done. It means possessing a spirit of leadership and perusing excellence, whatever the cost. And it also means knowing who you are and being proactive in making no apologies for walking in excellence. Yes, *The Chick in Charge* is flawed and fractured like everybody else. She is sometimes fragile, vulnerable and even weak. She faces fears, rejections and setbacks. However she does not give up when she is knocked down. In fact failure and disappointments usually strengthen her resolve. She is also swift, decisive, and determined. She is daring and disciplined enough to do the work, face the critics, and navigate the obstacles, whatever they are.

A lyric from an old Baptist hymn says, "A charge to keep I have, A God to glorify." We glorify God when we choose to walk in divine purpose and reflect His power in our lives. Purpose always links us to those in need of our love and service. My service happens to be in the field of security. I use it as a platform for ministry.

I hope my "Life Lessons, Business Principles, and Inspirational Tools" in this book inspire you to fully take charge of your life and make a difference.

CHAPTER ONE

A Case of Curiosity

The biggest adventure you can take is to live
the life of your dreams.
Oprah Winfrey

"I'M GONNA KICK YOUR BUTT!" MY AUNT REBECCA YELLED, AS SHE tried to grab me from behind my grandmother where I clung to the safety of her skirt tail as blood dripped from my nose.

"You hit that girl and I'm gonna break your dern face," my feisty grandma snapped back at my aunt. "You'd better keep your hands off her! Don't you see the child's nose is bleeding?"

I had just been caught spying on my young aunt and her boyfriend, Willie, who were smooching on the couch. Needless to say, my aunt was furious with me.

Every weekend, Willie would visit the house, and he and Aunt Rebecca would head straight for the couch in the "courting room," which doubled as a bedroom. I make no excuse about having a case of the curious, anxious to see what courting was all about and to understand why people did it. So one day, before the love birds made it to the room, I hid under the bed. My lively six-year-old mind didn't consider the fact that I might get trapped there for hours while they hugged and kissed and used sappy words to cuddle. I knew I'd get in trouble if Aunt Rebecca discovered me. So I stayed very still for what seemed like forever. But after I had heard enough of their noisy laughing, giggling, and smooching sounds, I wanted out.

Hurry up, you two, I gotta go to the bathroom soon. And just the thought caused me to almost wet on myself. Then, suddenly, I was hit with a severe case of nosebleed. Continuous droplets of blood trickling from my nose onto my lips and onto the floor caused me to panic, as my childish imagination kicked like a wild stallion. *I'm gonna die under this bed and no one will ever find me!* But it didn't matter. If I stayed I'd die, and if I got out from under the bed Aunt Rebecca would kill me. And sure enough, as I crawled out from my hiding place my aunt hit the roof! She didn't even stop to notice blood trickling down my face and staining my dress.

"Little girl, you're gonna get what's coming to you! You're always somewhere sneaking around. You have no business in our courting room. It's not a place for kids!" Aunt Rebecca yelled, trying to grab me. Her shouting drew grandma into the room. And with my ally near, I was ready to tattle.

"I just wanted to see what you two were doing," I shot back. "And Willie was patting your lap!"

This is when Aunt Rebecca lunged at me. "I'm gonna kick your butt…always sneaking around!"

The incident is hilarious when I recount it as an adult. But Aunt Rebecca was right. I was a very inquisitive, curious little girl. These traits, however, would serve me well in the business world, and in more ways than one.

If curiosity killed the cat, I'd be dead a long time ago. Ever since I can remember, I've been obsessively curious. It seems I was born with this extraordinary proclivity to pry, probe, and to always reason and ask why. My dear grandmother would lovingly say I was *"just plain nosey."* Other family members thought I was sassy and too opinionated for my own good.

18

The old phrase, "children should be seen and not heard," fell on deaf ears with me. I was that pesky child who tied adults up in knots with countless annoying questions. My mind was always restless. It was like a fidgety toddler squirming in the church pews, refusing to sit still during prayer, always disrupting Sunday service. Come to think of it, my whole life's journey has been one of disruptions, not the sort of disruption that causes chaos and confusion, but the type that takes charge, bucks the system, challenges the status quo, and defends the underdog.

One day at school, the underdog happened to be my cousin Willie Charles. And I was the fearless teenager who stood up to challenge the racist school yard bullies picking on Willie.

"We don't want no "niggers" at our school," one white student supposedly said, after they beat up Willie in the boys' bathroom.

When I got word of what happened I marched right inside the restroom and found a bruised up Willie shaken and scared to come out.

"We're going out of here Willie. Come on."

"But they are going to get me," Willie said, scanning the area.

"No, they are not," I assured.

I took Willie by the hand, and we walked to the top of the school steps where some students had gathered as spectators to the incident that occurred in the bathroom.

"If you want him, come get him!" I challenged.

But why did I say that, because within moments, a brief fist fight broke out on campus. But the gem in it all was that when it was over, Willie Charles had learned to stand up for himself.

I was also the young "upstart" who disrupted tradition at a major manufacturing plant in Michigan, and who, at the age of twenty-three, became the youngest black woman in upper management, supervising folks who were twice my age. Some of the old guards at General Motors (GM) were quick to caution me, like my dear friend Bill Wise—"Now Mary, I know you are ambitious and I know you'll do well. But I don't want you to bite off more than you can chew. This is a man's world, and they have been here a lot longer than you have."

But I had a sharp response to Bill and the rest of the men who thought they could put limits on me through intimidation.

"Well, Bill," I said, "that's okay. I am not afraid."

And I was the ambitious entrepreneur who shook things up in the highly competitive, white male-dominated Security Industry, never backing down until I became the best in the business.

How did I do it? God graced me with skills to disrupt BAU, or business as usual, and to achieve great success in the field I love. But it didn't come without a cost. I had to fight through obstacles to get it. I had to challenge and help change the "good old boy system" to stake my claim in the industry.

Now the fight is to keep the doors open and secure greater access for more women entrepreneurs who are eager to make their mark and ready to learn how.

The Security Lady

They call me the Security Lady. If there is something to know about protecting people, assets or environment, I know it or I know someone who does. It would be shameful if I didn't. I've invested thirty-five years of sweat, tears and hard work to blaze a trail in the security industry. And over time, dogged persistence has paid off. My company, ALL(n)1 Security, has grown much from a meager staff of one dreadfully overworked person—me. It's now an International security firm with more than three hundred highly skilled security professionals with offices in Georgia, Alabama, Mississippi, and Ghana, Africa.

The Bible instructs us not to despise humble or small beginnings. I am glad I did not. I started the business at my kitchen table, and in less than a month, moved into a three hundred square-foot office space, the size of a double walk-in closet. Today, ALL(n)1 Security takes up more than fifty-seven thousand square feet of office space in the same building. The first six months the company brought in more than three-hundred thousand dollars in contracts. By the third year, the company had shattered the million dollar ceiling. God was up to something big! Not only is ALL(n)1 a multi-million dollar company, it's the only nationally certified woman-owned "full-service" security firm in the country. Yes, full service. Long before we started offering more than security at special events, the company name, ALL(n)1, gave hint of a much larger, more sophisticated destiny. In addition to providing physical security, we specialize in personnel management, technology, and traffic control. We provide revolutionary security solutions to individuals, major corporations and government entities, schools, hotels, airports, just to name a few. In fact, if you ever park at Atlanta's Hartsfield-Jackson International Airport, ALL(n)1 Security protects you and your vehicle. We have been providing state-of-the art security service for the world's busiest airport since 2003. But building the business was sometimes a bumpy and turbulent ride. We had to continue to dream big, nonetheless.

Dream Big

Just about anybody who has an audacious dream to achieve greatness will face giants of resistance. You can either slay your Goliath or let him slay you. But Goliath can also be your greatest asset if you use resistance as a weapon to push you into destiny. I grew up in the Deep South, the cradle of slavery in America. Hundreds of years after the chains were broken and three million African Americans set free, the giants of resistance to fair and equitable treatment still roam the land. But so do the giant killers who are not afraid to fight for their right to succeed, and to succeed well.

I was the daughter of sharecroppers who lived in rural Mississippi. It's those crucial years that made me the giant slayer I am today in corporate America. My success as the first woman in the country to run a certified multimillion dollar, full-service security company is deeply rooted in the soil and soul of the south. For it is there, as a child, I developed the necessary character traits to stand up for myself and to later fight the giants of resistance to my personal and professional progress.

As humans, we are equipped with the primal urge to want to see what's on the other side of the proverbial fence, to push boundaries. This inborn curiosity caused me to wonder why things were the way they were, to search for explanations when none were given, and to feel compelled to right the wrongs when I recognized them.

As a child, I observed everything around me and paid close attention to adult conversations.

Act your age. Stay out of grown folks' business. These were the things adults around me would say when they would scold me. But it seemed like their reprimand was always followed by a friendly wink, a tap on the shoulder, or a twinkle of admiration in their eyes. *"This child,"* they'd declare with a chuckle, *"is different."* That acknowledgement only encouraged me to speak my mind more often and mimic my lively and very feisty grandma. My grandma had a sweet way of disarming people and taking charge when dicey family matters needed to be resolved.

Grandma lived just a stone's throw from our house on a dirt road that led to her front door. When I was about three years old, I'd walk the brief dusty path to visit her quite often. One day, it was she who made tracks to my house.

My mother had just had another baby, her third. I was my parents' second child. A new sister in the house meant I was no longer the baby at the center of attention. And you can imagine that there was even less attention to share when baby brother James joined the growing family. On top of it all, we were poor, and so was everybody else around us. My mom used flour sacs she saved from the general store to make some of our clothes. In the spring, we each got a new pair of flip flops, and in the fall, a new pair of tennis shoes. When we wore out the shoes mom would patch them together and insert extra shoe soles made of cardboard. If we outgrew them too quickly, she'd cut off the tops to make open-toe shoes so we would not have to go to school barefoot in the winter. Getting a pair of patent leather was a rear treat for special occasions, like church. Even water was scarce. We had to carry it in buckets from a neighbor's well nearby. All of us kids took a bath in the same water in a number eight tin tub. You can just imagine the film of dirt, grease, and grime on the side of the silver tub from four kids jumping in and out to bathe. And as more children kept coming, the little we had was stretched even further.

Eventually, nine of us—my parents, my maternal grandfather, and all six children lived in a two-room wood frame rented house in a sharecropping farming community in rural Mississippi. We had no indoor plumbing, but the family did enjoy central air and heating, just in reverse. Cracks in the walls and floors of our house provided oppressive heat in the summer and bone-chilling air in the winter.

Grandma didn't want me accidentally overlooked or starving for affection in this crowded two-room house, so she sort of adopted me. She figured my older sister, Mary Louise or Lou, was big enough to help mama with her growing brood. My younger sister, Bobbie, was too small. So I was deemed the "chosen one" who would go live with grandma. And I was ecstatic! I could not have loved another human being as much as I love my grandma. She showered me with affection, made me feel wanted and special. I got the personal attention I couldn't get at home. With grandma I felt like an only child. We often took short walks through the pasture between her house and my parents' house to help my mom with chores while she recovered from delivering babies. Grandma would fix a big dinner of cornbread, greens, and some type of meat for the entire family. I was her little helper delivering the meals.

"Come on, baby, let's get this food together so we can bring it to your mom and the kids."

"Okay, Gran, what do you want me to carry?" I'd say, eager to help.

"You take the bucket with the sweet tea."

We did this almost daily until my mother was able to get up on her feet and fully recuperate. When everybody was fed and the kitchen tidied up, Grandma and I would head back to her house across the pasture hand-in-hand and enjoy a very special bond.

My mother ended up having nine children in total, all delivered by midwives at home. Two of the last three brothers and sisters were born in what we called "the big house." This was the sprawling four-room rent house the family moved into to get some extra elbow room. Rick, the baby, was born after the family moved to another plantation.

As I grew, I'd spend the crop-picking months in the summer and fall at the big house being a bossy babysitter to my younger siblings and cousins. Believe it or not, I was just six years old when I started taking care of younger kids. And I did not like it one bit. My older sister Lou and I would fuss about it among ourselves.

"Momma is having babies every year," I'd complain. "If she keeps this up, she'll have twenty babies in twenty years."

"Yeah," Lou often agreed. "I wish they'd stop having so many babies. It's just more work for us."

But it was this adult responsibility that gave me my early lessons on leadership and taking charge. I lived in an era when young meant assuming your responsible role in the family. My parents worked in the cotton field. Well, my mother worked. My father was shiftless and often irresponsible. He had an eager thirst for illegal booze. Like so many men who felt trapped by an oppressive sharecropping system, my father turned to the bottle to cope. Most days, he stayed drunk on cheap moonshine whisky.

I can remember my dad stumbling home drunk and cursing the cows in the pasture along the way. "You big eye white faced heifers, all you do is walk and eat and poop all over the pasture, and I've gotta come through here stepping in all your sh__!"

When daddy got to the house drunk he'd be ready to lash out at anybody, including us kids. But one day, my mother was at her limits with his drunken behavior.

"Every time you come home drunk you want to start beating on these kids. I'm tired of it L.A.," my mom said. She had a way of making her soft voice sound stern.

I must have aggravated my dad the most, because it seemed that he always had me in his line of fire. It always bothered me, and I remember having a long talk with my grandma about it.

"Why do you think my dad doesn't like me? He likes all the other kids."

"It's not that your dad doesn't like you, baby," grandma tried to assure me. "He's drinking that liquor and having to go to the fields all the time. He's probably tired, or he may be drunk. But don't you worry, when you are with me, he's not going to touch you."

Our family was third-generation sharecroppers. We lived in a poor, rural community called Horse Pen, which was outside of Grenada, Mississippi. It's nearly one hundred and fifteen miles north of Jackson, the state capitol. I'd later poke fun at our small, tight-knit neighborhood, and jokingly describe it as an upscale, gated suburbia. The community sprung up on a long stretch of cow pasture surrounded by plantation land and endless rows of cotton fields. Only about five families lived there, mostly extended relatives. This gave us a sense of belonging and ownership, even though as renters, we owned nothing.

Ours was a gated community alright. We were gated in by a barb-wire fence, perhaps designed to keep us in our place. In my suspicious mind, it was meant to separate the haves from the have not's. The lighter skinned black sharecroppers just across the fence were the haves. They owned their land and some acted as though they were better than everybody else because they were "high yellow." We all know how that happened. Ask anybody with roots in Horse Pen, and they'll laugh and might tell you that, "Some white landowners couldn't resist the taste of brown sugar." In other words, late night dalliances with a few "colored "women left behind a few reminders with curly hair and light skin.

One landowner would later give his bi-racial children parcels of property to farm and to build their houses on. Although we all got along, I always felt like those neighbors across the fence had an unfair advantage. I probably resented it, too. It drove me to resolve never to end up on the poor side of the fence in life. So my seeds of self-determination and deep desire to succeed in life were planted on this simple premise.

I learned early on to think and reason on a level well beyond my age. This is mostly because I spent so much time with older people growing up. When they talked, I was like a sponge, soaking up every drop of worldly wisdom and perhaps a few foolish tales, too. The people who shaped my character and influenced me most in my childhood years were my paternal grandmother and step-grandfather. I spent a great deal of time shadowing each in different ways, developing a tight bond with both.

We called my step-grandfather Uncle T, because everybody in the neighborhood did. He and grandma encouraged my bold, fearless attitude and strong personality. With them, I was allowed to assert my childish opinions. So I never knew what "shy" meant. I was never afraid to express my ideas, argue my point, or chime in on "grown folks business."

"So, what do you think about us opening a little candy store here at the house, baby?" grandma asked one day.

"Oh, yes, Gran! I wanna be in charge!" I rattled off my suggestions and acted as though I was already running the operation. Little did we realize that this free reign was setting me up to later talk with ease to top politicians, CEOs of Fortune 500 companies, Hollywood celebrities, Heads of State in African countries, as well as the average, everyday person on the street.

"I bet you can't beat me this time Helen," dared my playmate Mac. Everybody called me by my middle name Helen, to distinguish me from Mary Louise, my older sister. Like Mac, some of the neighborhood boys often had a score to settle with me since I was a tomboy and very competitive. I was not one to shy away from a chance to beat the boys at their own game or get hurt trying. What also kept me occupied was my curious need to know "grown folks business." So while little girls my age were playing jump rope and baking mud pies in Horse Penn's rich, black dirt after school, I was kicking up dust somewhere else, often off on my own adventure. Some days, curiosity had me running breathlessly through the pasture just beyond the woods near my house. My anxious little feet hurried to keep up with Uncle T who was usually up to some mischief. I made it my business to stay on his heels to find out. I was Uncle T's faithful little tag-along. I knew where his illegal moonshine distillery was hidden just beyond the pasture in the woods. Perhaps the worst-kept secret in Horse Pen was that Uncle T was a bona fide bootlegger. It supplemented his meager sharecropper's income and helped him better care for his family.

It was fun to sneak off with him and watch Uncle T brew up his homemade whiskey.

"Why you digging holes in the ground, Uncle T?"

"Well, baby girl, that's how you keep the 'spirits' nice and cool once you bottle them up."

"Grandma says you're trying to hide your illegal booze from the law," I said with no bridle on my tongue.

"Yeah, that, too," Uncle T confessed quite nonchalantly.

I kept a very close watch on how Uncle T ran his clandestine operation. And I'd strain my eyes to make sure I'd remember the exact spots where he hid the inventory.

"Uncle T, why do they call it moonshine?" I wanted answers to anything my young brain could think of.

"Well, baby girl, that's 'cause we do all the whiskey making at night, under the light of the moon."

"I guess you can hide from the law at night, too, huh Uncle T?"

"That's right, baby girl, that's right. You're a smart little thing, ain't you? You pay attention to everything!"

The cheap liquor gave some people a quick buzz that made them giddy and feeling good. Others used the illegal booze to drown out despair, perhaps even depression. A whisk of moonshine offered some poor farmers temporary relief from the thoughts of their empty, unfulfilled life. As they picked cotton twelve hours a day under the sweltering sun, many of their hopes and dreams of a better life just shriveled away.

No matter how hard sharecroppers worked, some never got ahead, nor did they get out of debt. A robust and profitable harvest depended heavily on rain. Sharecroppers received stipends every month but were paid once a year and only if the harvest came in. Crop failure meant no pay. No pay meant families were forced to buy more necessary household items on credit at the general store. So the following year, farmers were not only working the fields to feed their family; they were working to pay back or "reclaim their soul" from the general store. It was not unusual for families to get trapped in this vicious debt cycle, just a whisper away from the chains that held our forefathers in bondage. One or two bad seasons could plunge a sharecropper deep into the chasm of economic slavery.

At age seven, I firmly decided that the sharecropping life was definitely not for me. Perhaps the defiant thought started forming in my young mind as I watched my mother go off to the field early every morning, to a place that would hold her for hours before allowing her to return home for good. Momma would make us breakfast of eggs and cured ham or salmon croquette, and then walk five miles one way to go pick cotton. At noon, she'd walk back home to check on us and prepare lunch for daddy and other relatives working the field. Then she'd walk back in the blazing sun, toting lunch on her third five-mile trip. You can imagine how tired and worn out she must have been by the time she made her final trek of the day. And to think, her evening chores as a wife and mother had yet to be tended to.

My mother was a quiet, reserved woman. But when it mattered, she'd raise her voice and firmly put her foot down. It happened one day when daddy suggested what she considered to be the unthinkable.

"You know, these three older girls are getting big enough to start going to the fields. If they chop a little corn or pick some cotton we'd make at least three or four extra dollars a week."

Momma cut him a look that could have curled the hair on the back of his neck. "You can forget that L.A.! My girls are not going to the fields. They are going to school! They are going to get an education, and they are getting up outta here." She just couldn't bear the thought of us having to live the same life she lived. Like every good parent, she wanted more for us. I knew I wanted more for myself, and my child-like mind figured out a plan after carefully observing the white folks who lived and worked among us.

Billy Frank James was the son of the white man, Curtis James, who managed the sharecroppers. He leased the parcels of track from the landowner and rented them to poor black farmers. For the most part, everybody got along. Young Billy Frank picked cotton alongside his black playmates. They swam together in the muddy neighborhood creek and played ball as equals. To this day, Billy Frank will tell you that life on the sharecropping farm was not so bad. But with his dad in charge, I suspect he didn't have to work as hard. And more than likely, he was paid more generously than the black cotton pickers. And the world was wide open to him.

The time came for Billy Frank to go off to college and "get an education." You could almost hear how a conversation could have played out between him and one of his old swimming buddies.

"Billy Frank, where you going all dressed up?"

"I'm getting ready to go off to college."

"Wish I could go, the black boy whispered under his breath as he hung his head. He knew he'd be forced to go to the fields to work fulltime now. He had no such options as Billy Frank.

I noticed that glaring inequity even as a young girl. And that's when I again, firmly fixed it in my little head that I was not going to the fields. I said to myself, I'm going to get a college education like Billy Frank, then I'll come back and run this farm. Yes, that will be my plan."

Billy Frank's leaving inspired me. So did his sister-in-law's arrival. Ramona was married to Billy Frank's older brother, Tootie. This young white chick was a sharp dresser, and every time Ramona came to Horse Pen, I'd take particular note of her outfits. She was as cute as a button and wore what must have been the latest designer fashions of the time. So I said to myself, *"That's how I want to dress, stylish like Ramona."*

So, my vision for myself at seven years old was to get a college education, dress stylishly, and eventually come back to the share-cropping farms in Horse Pen to run things. I wanted to be in charge, not spend my days shucking peas and picking cotton, or bootlegging like my step-grandfather, even though, as a child, I found what he did quite fascinating.

Everyone in town, except perhaps the authorities, knew Uncle T dabbled heavily in moonshine. And he had many regular customers bellying up for a swig of his corn liquor. It was like the family business, and Uncle T trained me well in it. As always, giddy curiosity got the best of me. I asked him a ton of questions about his brewing business.

"How come you use corn, Uncle T? What causes it to turn into whiskey?"

"Why do some people get drunk and some don't? Will I die if I drink some, Uncle T?"

Uncle T didn't seem to mind and loved the fact that I was a very fast learner. So, selling illegal moonshine marked my first lessons in entrepreneurship. It's where I cut my teeth on basic economics and money management. This was a fun way to learn math, even though I did not realize I was actually learning.

For three bits, or seventy-five cents, I'd pour a customer three ounces of liquor. So by default, practice or compulsory, I learned how to count cash, determine profit and loss, assess product cost per pint of liquor, broker deals with customers, negotiate sales, and make a profit. Since I knew where Uncle T hid his illegal booze, when he was away, his customers would come to me to buy a pint or two of booze. I felt so grown up and so in charge!

It's funny how no one ever snitched on Uncle T. There were rumors that he might have been supplying "the law" with moonshine in exchange for protection. Whatever the case, he got tipped off one day by the mailman.

"T, if you have any booze here at the house you need to get rid of it because "the law" is coming out to raid today."

"The law won't catch me," Uncle T bragged.

But in all actuality, the warning had given Uncle T just enough time to stuff all his supply of gallon bottle liquor in the trunk of his car and stash it away in some unknown location.

"Check the smoke house and the woodpile for some pint size. Oh yeah, and I got a stash in William and Robert's room. Let Helen show you," Uncle T yelled from his car to grandma as he sped off, blazing a trail to his mama's house to hide out.

Grandma and I hurried to gather up what was left of the illegal booze.

"Come baby, hurry, let's find a place to hide these," grandma said as she retrieved a few bottles from what I would have thought was a very unlikely hiding location.

This is when I discovered just how clever grandma was. My Aunt Josephine had just had baby and was sleeping with her new born on a mattress made of corn chuck.

"Roll over, Josephine, roll over."

"Help me stuff these bottles in this mattress."

"Why we gonna do that, gran?"

"Well, when "the law" comes and search this room, your aunty can start breastfeeding and they won't bother her."

"Oh," I said, as we both snickered like two sneaky criminals with the keys to their jail cell.

Sure enough, just as the mailman had warned, the police came to raid the premises. They searched every inch of the house during the raid and did not find one drop of moonshine liquor.

"We know he's got it around here. And we are gonna find it today," the officers kept repeating, growing more and more frustrated because they hadn't found anything.

They even looked under the bed where Aunt Josephine was busy breast-feeding her baby. They never found the booze, even though it was right under their nose. I was old enough to know what we did was wrong. But this was one time I kept my mouth closed.

If the police had caught and arrested Uncle T they would have treated him like a common criminal. But to me, he was a brilliant backwoods "brew master;" a clever chemist without a degree to authenticate it. I think Uncle T had to have had a high level of scientific skill to run his illegal whiskey stills. He had to be able to mix the right ingredients to get the chemicals to ferment and create his moonshine. Then he had to mitigate the risk of a fire if potentially explosive alcohol vapors escaped.

In addition to being a moonshiner, Uncle T was also a loan shark. He lent money to other families in the community who would fall on hard times. If the harvest was poor and the crops failed to yield enough profit, people didn't have enough money to get through to the next year. Because Uncle T, the bootlegger, had his side hustle, he always had extra funds. And since his supply was in high demand, he would charge extremely high interest rates for his "payday" loans. As you can imagine, a lot of his customers complained.

"Come on T, you know this rate is highway robbery."

"No sir, this is business. You want the loan or not?" Uncle T would ask, rather defiantly... Like his liquor peddling, Uncle T's loan sharking tactics were probably illegal, too. Come to think of it, everything Uncle T did was illegal.

Despite his outrageous rates, people in the neighborhood would set up a line of credit not just to borrow money but to buy his illegal booze as well. Especially vulnerable were men who just had to have a sip of whiskey during the week. Uncle T would gladly extend credit to them until they received their monthly stipend or got lucky at a crap shoot. The excessive interest alone should have sobered them up, but it never did.

So while running with Uncle T, I learned the other side of the law, the seedy and unsavory side. It made me street smart. This living incubator prepared me to be comfortable in any environment, and confident as a tough-as-nails business woman. I would sometimes warn people, *"Don't try to get over on me. Don't let this little soft voice fool you. I'm streetwise, and you don't want to take me on."* I would stand my ground among the country's top-level executives in my male-dominated business field. Just as I negotiated price deals while peddling Uncle T's moonshine as a child, years later I'd aggressively negotiate multi-million dollar security contracts with both confidence and a bit of southern charm.

My business skills were honed and polished through the best education, constant training and high-stakes sparring with my competitors. But they were first formed on the sharecropping farm in the sticks of Mississippi. That's where this "sassy" young girl was allowed to speak her mind, run a business, challenge authority, and refuse to be a pushover.

My grandma was the matriarch of Horse Penn, always the center of attention and the life of the party. She ran the neighborhood frolic house, which was her three-room house that was converted on the weekends. This is where folks went to shake off the worries of the week and dance their troubles away. Just about every weekend, the house was hopping with lively, foot-stomping jazz music. In every corner couples frolicked, stole kisses, and "got down" on the dance room floor until they were dripping with sweat from doing the Charlie or the Twist. Chuck Berry belting out, "Come on Baby" was hot back then. So was Otis Redding soulful song, "Sitting on the Dock of a Bay." All were just playful lyrics that danced in my head. Can you imagine being swept up in all of this unbridled exuberance? Every now and then, some playful adult, like my Aunt Rebecca, would whisk me up and twirl me around on the dance room floor.

"Come on, Helen, let's show them how to do the twist."

Some people laughed until they cried as they shook their bodies into all sorts of contorted shapes, mimicking drunken frolickers who had no rhythm but took to dancing anyway as liquor loosened their limbs and dulled their shame. At times, the atmosphere was so spirited, it felt like even the wood-framed house was swaying to the music, or were the weak floor boards cracking from the weight of the dancers it strained to hold up? A child's view of the world sometimes seem to be somewhat distorted.

The spirited party would spill onto my grandmother's back yard where drunken men rolled dice, gambled their money, and quarreled over their losses. There was lots of Uncle T's homemade liquor to keep the thirsty crowd tipsy and entertained. And what's a party without food? So of course, grandma always had chicken and fish sandwiches, sodas and her homemade dessert for sale. Frolic night was one of her most profitable streams of income. By now, you might gather that my grandmother was a hustler just like her husband, Uncle T, but in her own sweet way. And I watched and later mimicked everything she did, growing up in her shadow.

They called my grandmother Aunty Sugar because she was so sweet, loving, and compassionate. She canned fruit, cured ham, and gave away vegetables from her garden to anybody and everybody in need. But again, she was an astute businesswoman and always knew how to make and multiply a dollar. By the time I was in third grade, I was a big time product distributor, peddling cookies and candy at school for grandma. We ran a little retail store from the house, selling Moon Pies, Baby Ruths, Butterfingers, Almond Joys, all different kinds of sweet treats. She bought them wholesale from the candy man who visited the neighborhood once a month, and she sold retail to her customers. I went to her one day with an exciting business expansion proposition.

"Tell me what you think of this idea, Gran. I could take a bag of candy to school and sell them there. We'll make lots of money!"

It did not take much convincing for grandma to see the massive growth potential of our little enterprise. She was sold. Our goal was to make enough money to buy her most favorite thing in the world—new bedspreads every spring and fall.

Pretty bedspreads are the only thing I remember grandma ever asking for. During the spring and summer her beddings were a nice light blue, pink, or lime green with the white frills. In the fall season she'd switch them out to darker colors of russet and dark blue bedding. To this day, bedding is one of my favorite indulgences, thanks to grandmother's early influence. I will spend more money on bedding, sheets, towels and bedspreads than on designer shoes or pocketbooks.

As grandmother's little salesgirl, I carried a brown bag of candy to school, priced them at five cents a bar, and sold out nearly every day. I was determined that grandma was going to get her bedspread. I later increased distribution and profit by recruiting other kids to help me sell in exchange for a small cut. I did not realize it then, but I was learning business principles on how to hire, build a team, allocate and track inventory, and determine return on my (well, my grandmother's) investment or ROI. So when I say business is in my blood, yes indeed, it courses through my veins.

You see, my eagerness to create wealth, have my own, and design creative ways to run a profitable business was engrained in me as a child. There is no doubt in my mind that my early upbringing predisposed me to later succeed in business, no matter what field I chose. There was no question I'd be wealthy, do great things, and leave a legacy for my family. But I had to fight a few Goliaths along the way.

CHAPTER TWO

Change is Always Necessary

Nourish beginnings, let us nourish beginnings. Not all things are blest, but the seeds of all things are blest. The blessing is in the seed.
Muriel Rukeyser

WHERE ARE WE GOING, MA?" "BABY, WE ARE HEADED UP NORTH! I am so excited I could shout! Thank you, Jesus! We are gonna get a fresh start in life. No more of this god-forsaken, cotton-picking plantation labor, working for little to nothing. Daddy just got himself a job in Pontiac, Michigan working at that auto factory. Baby, we are getting up outta here. Thank you, Jesus!"

Scenes like this played out all across the south, as roughly six million African Americans relocated from the rural South to cities in the North, West, and Midwest between 1916 and 1970. It was part of the Great Migration. For many, it was the great escape from the back-breaking work of share cropping and picking cotton on former slave plantations. Entire families packed up their hopes and dreams to chase new economic opportunities, emerging industrial jobs, and an overall better way of life.

FROM HORSE PEN TO MICHIGAN

While in my early teens, I joined the mass exodus in the summer of 1968, but for a very different reason—to get away from my stern father who took a liking to beating me.

"Get your things and start packing. I'm sending you to live with your Aunt Mae and Uncle Homer in Michigan."

"What? Mama, are you serious?" I screamed so loud it would have shattered mama's fine china…if she had some. Nevertheless, it was a dream come true for me, because when I was much younger, I tried to get my aunt and uncle to adopt me. They had no children at the time, and with eight siblings, I often yearned to be an only child. I never felt as though I received enough love or attention from my parents.

Truth be told, I never quite bonded with my father. In fact, I never felt as though he liked me, even though grandma insisted he did. A childish mind had me convinced L.A. Robinson favored my older sister, Lou. She was his first born. And next, I figured he favored my younger sister Bobbie, who was the baby at the time. Who can resist an adorable baby? Consequently, Bobbie received all of the attention. I was the middle girl, stuck in between with no endearing distinction in the family pecking order, or at least that's what I imagined in my overactive mind. Perhaps it was because I mostly lived with my grandma and he never got to know me, or perhaps it was because I stood up to him more than any of my siblings did.

I remember the time he got drunk and turned his anger on my mother. Daddy kept a shot gun beside their bed, and when he went into his rages, he'd grab it. I'm not sure whether it was even loaded. But this particular night he came home drunk, and I made up in my mind that I was going to stick up for my mother and stand up to my dad.

"He's not gonna pull that gun on momma tonight," I said to Lou, as we both sat up in our beds, anticipating a forthcoming argument.

"So what are you gonna do?" Lou asked, sort of scared of what could happen to me.

While my parents were in the front room, or living room, I simply went into their bedroom, took the gun, and hid it in the outhouse. The next day, I took an ax from the woodpile and chopped off the handle of the shotgun. Daddy was never able to use that weapon again. He knew I did it, but he never confronted me about it. I was ready to take charge and risk his wrath when I thought he was wrong. To make matters worse, my sassy mouth would often land me in trouble with my dad, especially when I challenged authority.

I was barely thirteen years old when I publically defended my father's honor only to get my "butt whooped" for it. My dad and I had gone grocery shopping at Horse Pen's general store.

"Hey L.A.," the young white clerk said as we walked in the store.

Well, his frank rudeness got my blood boiling, addressing my father by his first name. It was disrespectful, and I was not afraid to tell him so. We, black kids, were taught to address elders, adults, and especially white folks, as mister or missus. Why did this teen feel it was okay for him to call my dad "L.A.?" So I challenged him with all manner of boldness.

"You know, you need to put a handle on my dad's name. You need to call him Mister L.A., because we have to call your dad Mister Billy," I said, in a daring challenge to the young clerk's action.

Well, my comment shocked the young store clerk into silence, and it infuriated my father. He was fighting mad as he yelled from across the store to me.

"Get over here!" Not only was he angry, he was scared, terrified that my speaking up would cause trouble. "Just you wait till we get home," he whispered, as he grit his teeth and grabbed my arm. "I'll take care of you when we get home."

"But I didn't do anything, I was just trying to defend you, daddy," I said, resisting his grip in protest. But for some reason, it seemed that no matter what I did I always got in trouble with my dad.

But I felt justified. Why shouldn't it be just as natural for young white kids to regard black adults with respect, as we had been taught to regarding white adults?

Looking back on it now, I doubt any other black child would have done something so bold as to notice the apparent disrespect, much more challenge a white person. Leave it to me to throw down the gauntlet and not care. There was, however, a painful price to pay for my boldness. When we got home, my dad beat my butt for defending him. But that whooping was the last straw, signaling a major turning point in my life.

Want to see a protective tiger mom pounce? Mess with her cub one too many times. That particular day my dad laid his hands on me caused my usually-docile mother to pounce.

"I am sick and tired of you beating on that girl. You are not gonna touch her again, because as soon as the school year is over, I am putting her on a train and sending her up North to Michigan."

"That's fine with me! That's probably a better place for her and her sassy mouth. If she stays down here she is gonna get herself killed and the rest of the family, too!" my dad shouted back, still fuming with anger from the grocery store incident.

No news could have been more thrilling to a precocious teenager. I was like a caged bird whose gate was about to fling open. Counting down the days till the final school bell would ring became my favorite pastime. *I'm going to Michigan to live with Aunt Mae and Uncle Homer!* I kept telling myself, as though I needed convincing.

I was so anxious to leave Horse Pen for greener pasture. No one could have been more eager to get off the sharecropping farm and kiss Mississippi goodbye, than I was. Yes, I'd miss my family. Yes, old childhood memories suddenly seemed more precious as I took a last stroll through the neighborhood. But I was anxious to make new memories in Michigan. Thoughts of no more beatings from my dad and no more nasty outhouses were enticing charms. Just the thought of taking a bath in a real bathtub made me giddy. I think my mind was racing faster than the Chicago-bound train on that fourteen-hour trip up north.

My uncle came to pick me up in his green and white convertible Chevrolet for the second half of my trip to Michigan. By then, I had already made up in my mind how my life would unfold.

The Underground Railroad

During the great migration, about forty percent of black southerners went to the big cities such as Chicago and New York. The rest populated secondary industrial cities, including Grand Rapids. This was where Aunt Mae and Uncle Homer had laid their roots. It was easier for them to relocate, since they had no children. The couple was the Harriet Tubman of the family. Their house provided rest and refuge to a steady stream of relatives traveling from the South who were in pursuit of economic fortunes up North. So we jokingly nicknamed the home at 1318 Sherman, the Underground Railroad. Over the years, more than ninety people stayed with Aunt Mae and Uncle Homer before relocating to other cities across the North and Midwest.

Grand Rapids opened up an entirely new and exciting world to me. Home was now in a mixed neighborhood. Whites and blacks lived side-by-side as apparent equals. My new high school was already integrated, unlike in Horse Penn where black and white students went to separate schools. But as some things changed others remained the same. It did not take me long to find a way to get my old business hustle on. And I could just imagine how proud my bootlegging Uncle T would have been.

"So Helen, you like gardening?" Aunt Mae asked as she smiled and handed me a pair of gloves just as I stepped out the back door.

"Well, it beats picking cotton, and it looks like a lot more fun."

We both chuckled. "You know, your uncle loves tulips and is raving about the new batch he just planted out front."

Aunt Mae and Uncle Homer were avid gardeners and kept the best yard in the neighborhood. So I jumped in the dirt and quickly learned how to cut grass and plant flowers. Pretty soon, I took over the landscaping duties myself. I'd cut my yard to perfection and then cut my neighbors' yards on either side of me, charging them modestly for my services. Before I knew it, I had a lawn care service that made me a tidy sum in the first summer. For me, hustling was instinctive, because from the early age of seven, I had been a keen student of business and finance. Finding creative ways to start a profitable side business was second nature to me.

It would surprise no one then, that high school extracurricular activities did not interest me a bit, except for the debate team. I found it far more gratifying to work part time jobs after school. That meant turning down a lot of offers to school parties. But since I worked so much, Aunt Mae would allow me to throw a party at the house every quarter during the year. Everybody in the neighborhood and all my school friends looked forward to it. It was like a block party with lots of food, loud music, and dancing in the basement under flashing strobe lights. My quarter parties were not as raucous as grandma's famous frolics. But like her, I was the main attraction and the life of the party.

But work came first. While my classmates went to the mall to hang out, I went to work. Throughout high school, I held jobs at four retail clothing stores and was a top sales person at each of them. I figured every bit of experience I garnered would help me "own my own" one day. I had not forgotten my promise to myself—*No share-cropping for me. I'm going to own the land and run things."* I had vowed to one day be *The Chick in Charge*, and Michigan gave me a clearer path to make it happen. My system for success was on track. Job opportunities were at every turn, I was chugging along in school with decent grades, and I had Aunt Mae to constantly encourage me. She reminded me so much of my dear grandmother. Even when her instructions were stern, they were always wrapped in love.

"Now Helen, You know you can do anything you set your mind to do. And Uncle Homer and I are here to help you. I expect you to do your homework, stay out of trouble, and definitely don't get pregnant, not on my watch!

We both laughed at that "don't get pregnant" warning. It seemed so far-fetched.

"That's one thing you don't have to worry about," I assured her. We chuckled again and then dismissed the thought.

I learned one of the most valuable financial lessons from Aunt Mae's wise counsel—saving. Whenever I got paid, she'd drum one mantra in my head—"Remember, dear, save at least ten percent of everything you earn."

This is what truly started me down the road to building wealth before I even knew what wealth building was. I also got into the habit of socking away all of my holiday and commission bonus checks. Being the top sales person at my store meant big bonuses. So, back in the early 1970's when I was sixteen or seventeen years old, it was not unusual for me to earn six-hundred dollars a month. I was so proud of myself that I couldn't wait for the first of every month to hand Uncle Homer a hundred and twenty-five dollars for rent. I'd catch him tootling in his mechanic shop behind the house.

"Here's my rent Uncle Homer, and you don't have to worry, I'm saving to pay for all my prom and graduation stuff, too." I was definitely taking charge of my life, and it felt good.

Later, I would learn the wisdom of tithing, and I added it to my giving routine. Taken together, it taught me independence, responsibility, and money management. It also taught me not to buy on credit.

If saving ten percent of my income was the number one piece of financial advice I received from Aunt Mae, number two was to never buy on credit. She would always say, *"Buy with cash, and whenever you take it home, is truly yours. No one can take it away from you."* To this day, I pay for everything in cash. My cars and my home are the only exceptions. There's nothing that I want or need right now that I've got to charge. If you check my wallet you'll find a Macy's, a Saks Fifth Avenue, a Home Depot and a couple other credit cards. Their sole purpose is to periodically circulate money in my accounts to increase my credit score.

I needed all the money I could stash away back in high school, because I had big, ambitious career plans. I planned on becoming a lawyer. I wanted to argue cases as a criminal defense attorney, which is why I joined my high school debate team. I wanted to practice and perfect my debating skills. Everything in my past and my personality confirmed I'd make an exceptional attorney. I candidly remember my high school guidance counselor cornering me in her office one day on the subject.

"Okay, Mary, make your case as to why you'd make a good lawyer," she said, sitting back in her chair with her feet propped up on her footrest.

"Well, for one, I'm nosey, well curious" I said, with a childish snicker. "I love to ask questions and press until I get answers, or drive people crazy trying. I love to argue and defend the underdog.

"Oh do you?" my counselor interrupted.

"Yes, someone has to. My family used to joke that I was too inquisitive, and that I was always in grown folks business, trying to argue a point."

My guidance counselor seemed impressed. I think I made my case that day.

I had plans to attend Michigan State University, but if it didn't work out, my backup strategy was to join the United States Air Force, become an officer and then an attorney once I left the military. I had my life meticulously planned out. But then a two-ton bomb fell and exploded all around me.

Almost overnight, my big dreams shattered into a million little pieces. I became pregnant. It happened during my senior year of high school, just four months before graduation. I was devastated.

The day I learned I was pregnant, I was a nervous wreck. I took the long, long way home, giving myself some time to think things through, at least that was my intention. When I approached the house, I was too afraid to even go inside. Instead, I walked back and forth on the front porch nervously wringing my hands as they shivered uncontrollably.

How can I tell Aunt Mae, how can I tell Aunt Mae? I kept repeating as I paced back and forth, rehearsing a line in my head that kept fading in and out. *She'll be so disappointed,* I kept telling myself. *So disappointed...Helen how could you!?* I was already drowning in guilt when Aunt Mae's haunting words came flooding back in my mind…"And you definitely can't get pregnant, not on my watch." With this haunting thought, my feet stopped moving, as though I was caught in quicksand.

All this time, my aunt was in the kitchen preparing dinner.

The shockwave that rocked my world in Michigan seemed to resonate as far away as rural Mississippi. I refused to even think about how the news must have hurt my beloved grandmother and disappointed my mom. On top of it all, I was embarrassed, humiliated, and deeply ashamed.

It wasn't long after, that Aunt Mae came to me and out of the blue asked, *"Are you pregnant?"*

The expression on my face spoke for me. Aunt Mae sat me down on the ledge of the bay window in the living room, gently took my hands, and looked into my eyes. She knew. I lowered my head.

"Look at me, Helen," she whispered, still holding my hands.

I sheepishly nodded yes and broke down in tears.

"Come, now…shhh. This is not the worst thing that could have happen to you. You are not the only girl to get pregnant in high school."

"Yes, but this was not supposed to happen to *me*!" I sobbed.

By now, I was lying limp in Aunt Mae's consoling arms, as she rocked me. She was suspicious all along. My excessive sleeping, the morning I got sick to my stomach and threw up, my constant craving for cinnamon hard candy and watermelon—all signs to the watchful eye that "a bun was in the oven."

For the first time, my life felt out of control. I felt I had brought shame to myself, my aunt Mae, and my entire family. *Why would my siblings want to look up to me now?* I wondered. I didn't think I was worthy of anybody's admiration. And what would happen to my plans to "go off to college and get an education" like Billy Frank?

It all seemed so unreal. I had just started dating my boyfriend, Robin, the year before. I was seventeen. He was six years older than me, was divorced, and had a child from his previous marriage. None of that had mattered though, because my aunt and uncle trusted him. He was the neighbor's nice kid they had watched grow up.

They thought he was safe, and that we were a good match. But in reality, all it really took was one night of unbridled, unprotected sex, and my future shifted under my feet. So instead of planning to go off to college or enlisting in the military, I found myself planning for an unwanted wedding and the arrival of a baby. My aunt begged me, however, to reconsider getting married.

"Sweetheart, if you don't want to marry him, you know you don't have to. Even though you are having a baby, you have a family who cares for you and will help you with your child," Aunt Mae advised. She believed getting married would only make a bad situation worse. Turns out, she was right. I wish I had taken her advice.

The birth of my daughter, Chana, three months later was the only bright spot in this unexpected, life-altering ordeal. I fell into depression afterward, as my rocky marriage quickly started falling apart.

I am not sure if I expected the rushed marriage to last, but I was hopeful. I even ignored the first sign of physical abuse before we said *I do*.

"Hey, hey, what are you doing hitting on Mary?" an old high school teacher said, intervening as he stumbled upon my fiancé slapping me in a parking lot outside of a wedding reception we had attended.

"This is none of your business. This is my woman," my fiancé said, so called defending his honor and manhood.

"No, you shouldn't be doing that, and I'm not gonna stand here and let you beat on her like that. You need to stop," Mr. Hopson said, not backing down one bit.

My soon-to-be husband backed off. He had accused me of flirting with the groom who was an ex-boyfriend of mine. I should have known then the man I was to marry was a jealous maniac. Still, out of pride, I would not call off the wedding—I didn't want to be labeled an unwed mother. The last thing I wanted was to be a single mother and for my daughter to be raised without her father. So at age nineteen, I married my daughter's daddy and quickly found myself bound to a man who was insanely jealous and excessively controlling. It was probably the saddest time in my life.

The failing marriage never stood a chance. We fought and argued constantly, especially when he tried to prevent me from going to college. The stress of being a new mom, in a new marriage, and in a new home with a husband who wanted to still run the streets and keep me under his thumb was unbearable. I was ashamed to call and complain to my family. I felt hurt, trapped and depressed, all the while losing my identity. The strong, fearless, self-determined young woman who went into the marriage had become a distant shadow of her former self.

For months, I languished in this stupor. Then I tried to rebound by enrolling in college, and when I did, all hell broke loose.

"Just where do you think you are going?" my ex said, jumping off the couch when he saw me with my book bag heading for the front door.

"I'm going to school. I have class today," I said casually.

"You're not leaving this house," he dared.

"Oh, yes I am," I defended.

My "defiance" and "back talking" really got to him this morning. He attempted to grab me by my neck. I jerked backward, and he missed.

"It's not gonna be a one-way fight this morning. You hit me, I'm gonna fight you back," I challenged. I dropped the book bag and positioned myself for the fight of my life.

He reached for me again, and I kicked him in the upper chest area, knocking him over the coffee table. The glass top of the table broke, and I quickly picked up a piece of broken glass and drew my hand back.

"Don't come near me again or I'll rip your head off with this glass," I promised. *"I want you gone from this apartment by the time I get back from school tonight."*

"Now, you really must be crazy," he said in both shock and disbelief.

But he must have seen something in my eyes that day, because he backed off, and he stayed completely away for about six months.

With the beat down my courage rose up, the incident clearly revealed another extension of myself, I still felt a sense of shame as a battered woman. For me, the shame was in the silence. I had seen my dad beat my mom, my granddad beat my grandmother, and I swore it would not happen to me.

Perhaps it was his way of trying to scare or intimidate me. But six months later, my estranged husband showed up at the house with his brother's gun. For some reason, instead of letting fear take over, I confronted him with a daring challenge.

"If you kill me, there ain't no jail or hell that's gonna keep the people who love me away from you. So the best thing for you to do is to kill yourself after you shoot me!" I said, staring him square in the eye. I must have scared my ex silly, because somehow the weapon accidently discharged and the bullet grazed his foot.

"See what you made me do!" he said, shocked by what had just transpired.

After a few more gut-wrenching moments of holding my breath as my ex examined his foot, he exited through the front door. I assumed he must have put me in the "she's crazy" category because he never bothered me again.

I took away two things from this experience. One being, that when you get yourself in deep trouble and realize only God can get you out, that's when, as the old folks would say, you get religion quick. Well, I got religion that day. I don't think I ever prayed so hard. I was so grateful to be alive. After my ex left the house, I just fell to my knees and kept thanking God for protecting me not only from my ex-husband, but from myself. I cannot definitely tell you what possessed me to defiantly threaten a man who came looking for me with a gun. Next, there was no question that God Himself, saved me from a dicey situation, and that He had to have some great plan for my life.

CHAPTER THREE

Business is Never Usual

*"It is not the beauty of a building you should look at; it's the
construction of the foundation that will stand the test of time."*
David Allan Coe

GREEK PHILOSOPHER, EPICTETUS, ONCE SAID, "IT'S NOT WHAT happens to you but how you react to it that matters." The game of life isn't always fair. No one said it would be. Sometimes, you won't recognize the eighty-mile-an-hour curve ball coming until it hits you between the eyes and knocks you out cold.

LEARN TO ADJUST

Life's setbacks are part of the necessary process. Mistakes can be your best teacher. They offer opportunities for personal growth that you would not otherwise have had. When my marriage ended in divorce, I reacted by applying the KIM principle; "Keep it Moving." I made no time to wallow in regret or dream of what could have been. I just stayed focused and kept it moving. I had regained my identity, and what mattered most was extracting the lesson from the pain, gaining wisdom born from the heartache, forgiving myself and others, and getting busy rebuilding my life.

I quickly jumped back into the workforce and continued pursuing my college career, but without the constant hassle of an insecure husband. This *Chick in Charge* had rediscovered her compass and was ready to chart a new course! Aquinas College provided the perfect backdrop.

I once heard that, "Obstacles are only opportunities in work clothes." So I got busy putting on my work clothes. This meant taking my daughter to school with me when I couldn't afford a baby sitter. It wasn't unusual to see me pushing a stroller on campus or adjusting a fidgety toddler on one hip while balancing a stack of text books on the other. Classmates who saw this struggling single mom probably took pity. I was focused on the opportunity to get an education, and nothing was going to stop me.

Aquinas College, a small Catholic college tucked away in the southeast side of Grand Rapids was a godsend. Often, the registration office where I worked doubled as a daycare. I was not ashamed to ask for help. And long before Hilary Clinton reminded the world that, "It takes a village to rear a child," my daughter, Chana, had benefited from the kindness of caring people on campus. It was nothing for my boss, Sister Elizabeth Eardly, to keep an eye on Chana while I dashed off to a class.

There was one subject I didn't need to be introduced to in college—Hustle 101. Uncle T. had taught me all about hustling back in Horse Pen. His business "degree" was earned through his struggle. He hustled to take care of his family and supplement the pittance he received from picking cotton. Selling moonshine liquor and operating as a loan shark was shady business. But it birthed his skills as an entrepreneur. I, too, had mastered the hustle, which means to move on a business or money-making plan energetically. And there were plenty of opportunities on campus for an enterprising hustler like me. It didn't take long for me to set up a profitable operation with college classmates as my clients.

Find a Need and Fill It

When I heard my friends gripe about the food to the Black Student Union, I knew it was time to get my hustle on.

"Hey guys, I'll whip you up a home cooked meal at my house. Any takers?" I challenged.

"Really, what do you mean?" asked one of my friends.

"You guys buy the groceries, and I'll cook your favorite meals at a reasonable charge, of course."

"How soon can you make some jerk chicken?" my West Indian friend, Dena, yelled out.

And that marked the beginning of a sweet business deal with my college friends. I was the only one with an off campus apartment, so it quickly became the regular hangout spot.

"Oh, and I heard some of you fussing about having to go to the laundry mat to wash your clothes. I can cover that, too," I added.

So we had an agreement; the guys paid for the groceries, and I did the cooking. The girls who came over got to use my washer and dryer, under the condition they brought their own laundry detergent, did my laundry, and babysat my daughter for free. This tidy little business arrangement helped me save money and pay rent during the two and a half years I spent at Aquinas College.

Studies show nearly half of America's college students drop out before they get their degree. Count me in that number. I left Aquinas College in my junior year. Back in my day, the dropout rate was not as high as it currently is. What was high and lofty was my plan to land a job at General Motors, the giant carmaker based in Michigan. And if that meant leaving college early, so be it. Parental responsibilities prompted me to explore another avenue to success. But getting a GM job without inside connection was tough.

Nepotism guarded the entrance door. The "good ole boy" system made sure relatives of GM workers got a shoe in on any job. Such blatant favoritism was woven into the culture of the manufacturing industry, period. And union-strong companies, like GM, that helped drive the nation's economic engine during the industrial boom, were no exception. I had no family members working at GM to pull a few strings or drop my name. So when I got a chance to clinch a lowly entry-level summer job at the plant I jumped at it.

Pam Jones and I met the day I went to GM to fill out my job application. She was a student at Michigan State and was looking for summer work. I was looking for a career. One day, we had a brief conversation, trying to gauge one another's intentions. "Girl, if you get this job, are you going back to school?" Pam asked. "No. I'm going to have a career here," I confidently responded. "Are you kidding, you're going to work at this plant?" "Yes. What are you going to do?" I asked, curious to learn of her plan. "Oh, my mom and dad would kill me! I have to go back to school. So I can only work this summer." Pam had parents and a built-in support system. I was a single mom with a hungry mouth to feed. My daughter, Chana, was about four years old by now. Yes, college would have to wait. In my mind, GM was almost like college. My strategy was to capitalize on the skills and training GM was known to offer its employees. Soon, ideas started to percolate on how I could quickly move up the ranks and into management. I was intent on making my "affair" with GM more than just a summer fling.

Pam and I were hired as hourly precision grinding operators. After a few days on the job, we engaged in another conversation, our way of deciding whether our goals had quickly changed. "Girl, are you going to keep doing this grinding?" I asked. "Well, that's what we are hired for," Pam said, obliging to the mundane task we had been assigned. "Maybe that's what you were hired for. But I want Don Monroe's job," I said, having already determined I wanted something bigger and better for myself.

Don Monroe was my supervisor. And from day one, I had my

eyes fixed on getting his position, or one like it. As you can see, boldness has always been one of my strong suits. I was ready to take a gamble and risk, sounding ridiculous or even pompous. After just one week on the job, I approached my boss.

"Don, I want a supervisor job like yours. So tell me, how can I position myself to make it happen soon?

Don Monroe had worked on the floor for thirteen years before he got promoted to supervisor. So no wonder he laughed in my face and shrugged me off. "It's not gonna happen," he said, matter-of-factly.

But little did Don know, that a "no" to me is like extra engine fuel to power my persistence. For several weeks, I nagged Don.

"Go talk to your boss," I urged him. "Tell him how eager I am to join his management team. They need me," I persisted. But Don would not budge, and I was running out of time.

I remember learning during orientation, that after sixty days on the job, a new GM worker would automatically become a union member. This meant paying union dues. This was not going to work for me. *Why do I need a union to speak for me and I am perfectly capable of representing myself?*

The only way to avoid being "drafted" into the union was to get a management position within the sixty-day window. So with time ticking I ratcheted up my determination.

I did not care if my boss saw me as a cocky overachiever. It didn't matter that I was "with GM for barley two weeks and knew hardly nothing about the plant," as my supervisor made abundantly clear. I was always a fast-learner and excelled in whatever I put my mind to. So I was sure I could perform well in a management position, given the opportunity. So what is a girl to do when the door leading to destiny is slammed shut? Follow my lead—don't walk away in disgust and defeat but find a way to go around the obstacle. And that's exactly what I did. I went directly to my supervisor's boss, Buzz Bailey.

"You've got to be out of your mind. Ain't no way in hell they're going to hire a young black woman to be a supervisor. And you're cute too? That's not what you want to do," Buzz Bailey said to me, looking me up and down.

But I wanted the education, and I wanted the management training, so I conveyed my intentions to him.

"That's exactly what I want to do. And I don't want you to make that decision for me. Just tell me what steps I need to take because I'm trying to get into GMI."

GMI stands for General Motors Institute, an in-house school established in 1926 to train GM plant managers, supervisors and engineers. It grew to offer extensive courses and a strong cooperative education program. GMI became so successful that, by the 1990's, it later became Kettering University, a fully-accredited school in Flint, Michigan.

Getting into GMI had become my new number one goal. A co-op work study would enable me to gain invaluable career training while I worked at the plant. By now, I had been at the plant for forty-five days. That left me only fifteen days to convince the powers that be to switch me into management. So I kept up the pressure. This time, I pushed my way into the plant's superintendent's office. If that door had slammed in my face, too, I was prepared to appeal to the plant's top man—the CEO himself.

This is precisely what it took. My persistence impressed CEO so much until he made a call to the superintendent.

"I don't know how you guys missed this, but anybody who has been in this plant less than forty-five days and has the courage to come to my office is someone you should have on your team. I am sending her back to you for you to make the decision."

My advice to you—Persistence always pays off.

In lightning speed the superintendent enrolled me in a twelve-week management training program. I was the youngest leadership trainee and the only person of color in the class. The other trainee candidates were probably twice my age and had already had ten to fifteen years of experience at the plant. I had about four months. So, imagine what they were all thinking when I showed up on the first day of training.

The fact that I was daintily dressed and very lady-like turned a few heads. In fact, several of the senior trainees approached me.

"You really think you want to be a supervisor?" one of the management trainees asked.

"Excuse me?"

"Well, it's just that a plant supervisor's job is strenuous work and you, well—." he said, trying to soften up the underlying tone.

"Good Morning everyone!" I said as I waltzed into the training room, which was hardly what they expected. I guess I looked more suited for a delicate secretary job in the CEO's office. But looks can be deceiving. Little did they know I grew up with an auto mechanic and got my share of grimy engine grease under my finger nails from helping my Uncle Homer pull apart and reassemble car parts. Convincing them of my ability would take some doing.

After the classroom training, I was put on the plant floor for twelve weeks of hands-on training as a manager. It was "do or die" time. To make matters more challenging, I was assigned the worst department with what I considered the most people. This is how my career at GM began—with a tall order. It was now my job to manage the almost 70 people of Department 962. I was just twenty-four years old. Ready or not, I had to take charge.

My department's task was to grind the inside of the valve lifter which was a part of the fuel injector. Our daily output was among the highest in demand at the plant, since what we produced was so crucial to the forward movement of the assembly line process.

The welcome committee didn't show up to greet me when I came on board to supervise this big operation after only four months at GM. Some older veteran workers were livid. Others stood by waiting for me to fail. Many were eager to test my leadership skills. I had five skilled tradesmen assigned to keep all of our equipment and machinery going who just sat and looked at me. I could almost read their minds.

"So who do you think you are, Miss Upstart? What could you possibly know about manufacturing and operations?"

One of the biggest tests of my management competency came early.

When I took over as supervisor my manufacturing department was wasting time and a lot of money because something was wrong in the production line process. Having to scrap and rework was costing us more than a million dollars a week. No one could figure out what was causing it. Of course my inquisitive disposition wouldn't let me rest until I identified and resolved the matter. I became obsessed with trying to identify the root cause. I figured we had to thoroughly examine our machines to determine whether our department was indeed responsible for the problem, or whether the occurrence originated in an up-line before the parts were transferred to us for precision grinding.

So I posted a worker on the lookout for any union types. Then, I rolled up my sleeves, slipped on a pair of gloves, and slid inside the grinding machine. Then I phoned Uncle Homer.

"Uncle Homer, we have a problem here at the plant with the grinding wheel. Can you walk me through some troubleshooting?"

For years, I had watched Uncle Homer do brake jobs and swap out engines. So I was very familiar with the basic functions of mechanical tools and how equipment works. On his advice my team and I re-tested the grinding wheels and other operational parts, which seemed to all be in sync.

Uncle Homer walked me through troubleshooting steps, and as it turned out, the trouble was in the steel, having come into the plant defective. So the bad stock was causing breakage, waste, and costly reworks.

Had it not been for my team's aggressive, hands-on approach to pinpoint the problem, it is quite possible that the problem would have lingered, causing further damage and fiscal loss. For anyone who ever doubted otherwise, this incident proved that *The Chick in Charge* was more than just a pretty face.

TURN OBSTACLES INTO OPPORTUNITIES

Being handed the worst department that was wasting money on the product line was perhaps the best thing that could have happened to me. It forced me to jump in with both feet as a young leader, take charge, and become an avid problem-solver. It also meant fostering relationships, forming effective teamwork and wooing over the union, which could shut me down if they did not agree with my methods.

General Motors taught me how to make potential enemies and agitators my friends, or at least keep them close by. You can't excel in a male-dominated environment by having a reputation of "not playing nice with others," or trying to be Super Woman. Some of the most valuable lessons I learned at GM were from my white male colleagues in management or with the union. I was never afraid to ask for help. I readily sought their counsel and advice.

Ray Winoweicki became one of my most loyal advisors and a great friend. But he started out as a potential foe. Ray cursed like a sailor and had serious issues with blacks and women, of which I am both. He shut me up fast when I tried to get to know him.

"I told you I don't like blacks and I don't like women. The only female I like is my dog."

What do you say to that? As a union set-up man, Ray was responsible for keeping our equipment running and providing mechanical support. I wanted to learn how the machine operated, but he'd refused to train me. Union rules restricted managers, like me, from running the equipment. So forming a relationship with Ray was crucial, and I had to get past his reputation as a racist in order to befriend him. So I planned a strategy to win him over.

Ray had a big belly and a long white beard. My routine was to walk over to Ray, pat him on the belly, jerk his beard, and strike up small conversation.

"Ray, you know that I am not going anywhere," I said one particular day.

"Don't be too sure about that," Ray cautioned.

"I am sure about one thing, and that is that you are going to keep me here, because we are going become best friends."

"The hell we are," Ray said, his eyes widening.

"Yep, you just watch"

This little routine happened more than once. I didn't stop with just conversing with Ray. I noticed he drank black coffee. So I'd go to the vending machine and get two cups of coffee, one for him and one for me. I'd give him his cup of coffee and he'd start drinking… and I'd go right back into a pre-orchestrated conversation.

"You know what I need, Ray."

"You are not gonna get it."

After a while, Ray started to warm up to me. I didn't just stop there, I discovered what was of interest to Ray and built conversations around these topics. I learned details about his family and wove those into our talks. When he least expected it, I'd swoop in again with what I needed from Ray. One of our conversations revealed that I might have won Ray over.

"Are you ready to train me?" I said, trying to gauge his commitment.

"You know the union is not going to allow you to work this equipment."

"I'm not working if you are training me, Ray."

"How are you going to get away with that?"

"Well I'm not sure—but I bet you'll figure it out."

"Well, you know you have to put some gloves on. And let me go see if I can find an apron for you."

It took me about two months to break down the wall of resistance and build a trusting relationship with Ray. The fact that I was able to turn the roughest, meanest guy into my good friend gave me serious "street credibility" at the plant. Just imagine the looks we got: the sassy young black chic and the ornery white "racist" hanging out. Ray became a valuable source and my extra pair of eyes and ears on the manufacturing floor. He would keep me informed of anything that compromised productivity.

Ray also taught me how to handle grievances with people in the department, even how to strategically resolve dicey matters with the union, and how to make union bosses my friends. I took advantage of his thirty years of experience at the plant to learn the system and the tricks of the trade in order to fast-track my own progress.

I couldn't convert all my "enemies" or critics. But I still applied the kindness principle. For those who despised the "young uppity black chic," I just killed them with kindness.

Jesus Christ once instructed us to, "Love your enemy, and bless those who persecute you." But why? It's an ingenious counter move. When you respond to hate with love, it confounds and disarms your enemies. And then we must wrangle with our own inner demons. Many people, however, let fear, ego, or their own prejudices isolate them in the workplace. They don't want to appear vulnerable in an environment where they might be the only female or lone black person. But being intimidated in life or in business can stunt your growth and forward movement. The best way to shake it is to come to the table with problem-solving ideas and show results. That's one of the secret weapons of being a *Chick in Charge.*

At the end of the twelve week management training some supervisor-trainees went back to doing hourly factory work. They didn't make the cut. The prissy twenty four year-old who didn't fit the traditional mold of a department "boss" was still standing. And I learned to serve in order to be served.

On a daily basis, direct and personal contact was my management style. I got to know my workers one-by-one, name-by-name. I made it my business to learn about their families, their birthdays, and their personal struggles and took note of what mattered to them as human beings. In supervising Department 962 for two and a half years, I won their trust and loyalty. Somewhere along the way, resistance to my age, gender, or race faded in the distance. What spoke volumes was my ability to take charge of situations, find solutions, produce results, and inspire my team to do the same.

CHAPTER FOUR

Define Your Success

*Do not go where the path may lead, go instead where
there is no path and leave a trail.*
Ralph Waldo Emerson

WHAT DO YOU DO AFTER YOU HAVE CONQUERED THE WORLD? BY
1977, I felt I had arrived in life, becoming one of the youngest
female supervisors at GM. At age twenty-six my supervisory salary
was roughly fifty thousand dollars a year. When adjusted for inflation,
the salary is equivalent to two-hundred and fifty thousand dollars
today. But it wasn't enough. My success at GM did not come with
satisfaction guaranteed. No matter how high I climbed up the
corporate ladder I still had to punch the clock, and was still just a
worker, not the owner. True, my salary was light years ahead of what
my sharecropping parents could have ever dreamed of earning. But
how far had I really progressed? I had traded Horse Penn's farming
plantations for a manufacturing plant that offered a good living.
Indeed, it was progress. Like my parents, my skills were being used
to help someone else grow their business and help someone else get
rich. My entrepreneurial spirit that sprouted as a child started to stir
inside. I knew deep down that GM was only part of the process to
drive me to my ultimate destiny. It was clear working at GM was a
training ground to hone my leadership and business skills for later
use. What that later use would be was still foggy, however.

Ancient Rome's most famous leader, Julius Caesar, once said, "I came, I saw, I conquered." His brief report of a military victory captured my sentiment at GM, of getting a supervisory position. I led the charge to stop the financial hemorrhaging in my department and cut millions of dollars in losses while winning over most of my skeptics and clinching the loyalty of my workers, even the union bosses. *I came. I saw. I conquered.* Now, a new challenge had me restless and itching. So I decided to put my fifty-thousand-dollar job on ice and request a one-year educational leave of absence from GM to self-reflect and breathe in some fresh air. Educational leave was one of the great company benefits. It was likely not designed as an escape, which is what I used it for, however. And what better place to escape to than to the windy city of Chicago, which was about one-hundred eighty miles south west of Grand Rapids.

THE JOURNEY

"Come on Mary, you know we gonna have some big time fun! Darling, you have not lived until you have lived in the windy city." "Slick Smitty, you know you always have a way with words," I laughed as I teased my DJ friend as we gabbed on the phone.

It was Smitty's enticing description of the night life in Chicago that finally convinced me to move there with him. He promised it would be an adventure, and that's exactly what I was looking for. So just like that we were off to have unbridled fun in the windy city.

Smitty soon taught me his mobile DJ service business and, quite naturally, I insisted on becoming his business partner. In no time, we were DJ-ing at parties and events all over Chicago almost every weekend. My one-year "educational" leave of absence turned into a nearly four-year stint of partying and trying my hands at various fun jobs.

I did a little modeling for a new-found designer friend, "ClaRissa" with Fashion Moves Chicago Style. She had fashion pieces in the famous Chicago-based Ebony Fashion Fair. This traveling fashion show featured mostly African-American models on the runway. It showcased African-American designers as well as iconic European designers such as Givenchy, Oscar De La Renta, and Yves St Laurent.

For more than fifty years, the Ebony Fashion Show crisscrossed the country. It visited more than two hundred cities in the U.S., Canada, and the Caribbean. It raised tens of millions of dollars for African-American charities. The event was the brainchild of Eunice Johnson, wife of John Johnson and co-founder of Johnson Publishing Company. Their flagship product was Ebony Magazine, which was a source of deep pride in the black community. Since 1945, Ebony has celebrated African-American history, culture, celebrities, politics, and highlighted great accomplishments.

Chicago's intoxicating social vibes of black fashion, style, and culture only served to boost my already healthy appetite for living large. Black pride and black beauty were elevated higher when Mrs. Johnson created Fashion Fair Cosmetics. It was a cosmetics line just for "us" to compliment her world-famous fashion show. And not being one to ever shy away from trying something new, I became a make-up artist for the company.

No one connected to the frenzied high-drama and flamboyancy of the fashion industry could walk away unscathed. This is where I picked up my penchant for designer clothes. Years later, I still have a hard time shopping off the rack at a department store. Having designer friends that made my tailored outfits for little or nothing had spoiled me rotten.

My Ebony Fashion Fair connections landed me a bumper crop of clients when I tried my hand at selling hosiery out of my apartment. I'd buy my wholesale inventory from a Chinese distributor for fifty-cents a pair and then sell them at one dollar and fifty cents each—a one hundred and fifty percent profit.

But play time had to end. I finally got around to completing a business course to satisfy my educational leave from GM. I then worked for my instructor as a bookkeeper in his small business.

My Chicago excursion might seem frivolous to some, but those side jobs equipped me with a wealth of knowledge and insight on customer care and wholesale distribution, although none of these fun distracting side gigs allowed me to make the type of money I made at GM. They could not afford me the lifestyle I had grown accustomed to. So I gave up my days of partying and living on "the wild side" in Chicago. After almost four years, I returned to Grand Rapids.

"I'm back, you all," was my proud declaration as I stepped onto the assembly floor for the first time in a long while.

Now, who would have the audacity to go request their old job back after turning a one-year authorized leave into nearly a four-year leave? That would be me. The saving grace was I had kept in touch with my boss, stayed on stand-by if he needed me, and didn't burn any bridges. The company, however, was under no obligation to keep my job open. But I stepped right into General Motors one day and announced I was back. The company rehired me on the spot! They reinstated my supervisory position at the same pay rate and with full benefits. I went back to work the following day. Call me foolish, but I believe what the Bible says, "You have not because you ask not."

You could be missing out on a business breakthrough because you are too scared to ask. Ask the bank for that loan. Ask the client for your full fee. Ask the company for the big contract. Ask your boss for that promotion. What do you have to lose? You'd be surprised what divine favor awaits you.

Call me crazy. But I also believe divine favor has followed me like a "pillar of cloud." It was the same providence that protected the children of Israel during their years of wandering in the wilderness. At that point in my life, I too was wandering through my own wilderness. But God had a plan. And it turned out that my second stint at GM was just a brief layover.

There were no fixed supervisory posts available when I returned to GM. So I was used as a swing supervisor. This meant relieving vacationing plant supervisors. It was only a matter of time before the assignment fizzled, and I had to land somewhere in the company. This would prove to be another critical turning point in my life. The notion of security work was about to enter my thought for the very first time.

You never know what magic you can create if you just snoop around and ask the right people the right questions. My first job as a security guard was never posted on a company website or published internally. That's because the job never existed. I created it right there at GM. While making the rounds one day during my time as a swing supervisor, I noticed new construction going on at the plant, and nosey me went snooping for information.

"Hi there, it seems like something big is happening back here. What's with all this construction? I asked, when I ran into the construction manager.

"Well, GM is expanding the shipping and receiving area of the plant."

"Oh," I said, with growing interest. I probed further, learning that all shipping and receiving items would come through one gate. With this information, I saw an opportunity open up before me, and my hustling instinct kicked in.

So I quickly went to the personnel manager and asked, "Don't you think you'll need some security for the new expansion project?" I said, pausing for a moment while awaiting her answer. But she seemed to be taking too long to respond, so I continued with, "If you need someone to overseer security there, you are looking at her."

It was a bold move, but I leaped at the new opportunity. Mind you, never once in my life had I entertained the thought of working security. So, it had to be a God idea that had dropped in my spirit. I just ran with it.

Since the clock was running out on me as a swing supervisor, I figured what did I have to lose? Why not work as a security guard? And this is how I stumbled into the security industry more than thirty years ago. I did what most people wouldn't. I saw an opportunity and was bold enough to ask questions. I offered a solution to a potential problem, and it created a job. It was this one job that proved to be the catalyst for a career that turned into a multi-million dollar security business. It took stepping out and being forward-thinking and proactive.

BE PROACTIVE

How proactive are you? Rear Admiral Grace Hopper coined this famous phrase, "It's easier to ask forgiveness than to ask permission." Great leaders like her don't wait to be asked. They find what needs to be done. Then they take charge of getting it done. Admiral Hopper worked for the U.S. Navy as an early computer programmer. She is credited with leading the team that programmed the first computers. This Rear Admiral was *The Chick in Charge* in her male-dominated world. In fact, in 1969, Hopper was awarded the first ever Computer Science "Man-of-the-Year" Award from the Data Processing Management Association. Her skills were so progressive and her leadership qualities so valued that the Navy called her out of retirement when she was sixty years old.

Hopper once said, "Humans are allergic to change. They love to say, 'We've always done it this way.' I try to fight that. That's why I have a clock on my wall that runs counter-clockwise." Imagine that!

Becoming a security guard to watch trucks pick up and deliver equipment was new and different, but soon it was not enough for me. I started fishing for ways to improve the security operation. This is when I discovered certain inefficiencies and brought them to my new boss' attention. Like Admiral Hopper, I am solution-driven and seldom ask permissions. In this instance, I wrote a detailed proposal to my boss, Roger Penske, who had purchased GM's diesel operation. The proposal outlined possible fixes to the faulty security procedures. Surprisingly, Mr. Penske accepted my proposal and decided to upgrade the security program using the suggested strategies in my proposal. Nearly one hundred people applied for the job to set up the new system. But because it was my idea and my proposal, I got the job.

Once again, by being proactive, I created an opportunity that led to a huge promotion. In no time, I was security coordinator. That day in 1988 started my career as an executive in the Security Industry. I was only thirty-four years old. In reflecting back, I was grateful to have grown up in a place called Horse Pen, Mississippi. I was thankful for Grandma and Uncle T—they had encouraged me to boldly speak my mind when it mattered. Watching them, I learned to take the lead when leadership was needed and to find solutions instead of just complaining about a problem.

My career was now on a non-stop bullet train running at maximum operating speed. The big day came when I was named Director of Security. I buckled down and started consuming every morsel of available information in the security industry. I was ravenous! I took every class and every course and attended just about every security conference offered. I soaked up specialized training for the fire brigade, occupational health services, anything I could get under my belt. This is what overachievers do. And for three years, I excelled at my job. As always, I went above and beyond the call of duty as director. Then one day, in November of 1991, out of nowhere, a second two-ton bomb struck my life and knocked me off my feet.

"Mary, I need to see you my office this afternoon around one thirty," my boss said to me, matter-of-factly.

"Not a problem Sir. Anything I need to prep for?"

"No, oh no." he said.

I never gave it much thought what the meeting could be about until I stepped into his office and noticed the Human Resources Department director was seated in there. I had the feeling that I was about to be served up quite a surprise.

"Mary, the company is making some changes, and we are moving you to the HR Department. Now, I know this comes as a surprise. But we need to train you as an HR specialist."

"What? I said, finally coming up for air after my boss' words had almost suffocated me.

"Is it my performance?"

"No, no. You are an outstanding Security Director. We just feel it's time to cross-train all our executives."

This meant I was now assigned to a lower-paying job in HR. And it didn't matter to them that I had no background in Human Resources.

It was no time to panic or cry foul. After gathering my wits, I turned to my boss and gave him a proposition.

"It's obvious I don't have a choice, but I'll give it six months with one condition."

"I'm listening," he said, anticipating what the condition would entail.

"You will allow me to get all the training I need to be effective as an HR specialist.

"Okay," he agreed, nodding his head simultaneously.

"And after the six months, if I still don't like it, you'll reassign me as Director of Security here."

"Sounds fair enough."

"If you don't, I will pursue directorship somewhere else or I will start my own company."

"Agreed," said my boss.

And the meeting was over before I knew it. I was thirty-eight years old, and my life was about to take a hard turn with unpredictable heartaches and unavoidable challenges.

CHAPTER FIVE
Learn to Adjust

Here is the prime condition of success: Concentrate your energy, thought and capital exclusively upon the business in which you are engaged. Having begun on one line, resolve to fight it out on that line, to lead in it, adopt every improvement, have the best machinery, and know the most about it.
Andrew Carnegie

IT WAS MY BABY BROTHER, RICK ROBINSON, WHO LURED ME INTO becoming a Georgia peach. He knew I was dying on the vine in Michigan. I had just been demoted from my Director of Security position. So needless to say, I was restless and unhappy.

"Helen you gotta move to Atlanta!" Rick sounded ecstatic during a phone conversation we had in 1992.

"This is your type of town, Sis. The energy of the city definitely suits that carefree personality of yours."

Rick assured me I'd have no problem making friends and finding great business opportunities. He had recently left Grand Rapids in search of greener pastures himself, as he pursued his education at Clark Atlanta University. He wanted a break from the stoic, industrial Midwest, with its thick plant factory atmosphere. Immediately, he was struck by Atlanta's vibrancy and thought I'd fit right in. And fit in I did. But I must say, for the first time in my life I felt a bit intimidated. I was accustomed to being a stand-out, a maverick, or the main *Chick in Charge* wherever I went. Atlanta was already brimming with a sea of savvy, successful and forward-thinking business women. This was the norm, not the exception.

I jumped in with both feet, ready to pan for gold in "The Black Mecca." Within months of arriving in town, a colleague and I started my first security company, CASS Security. My partner kept his full-time corporate job. So the lion-share of day-to-day operations fell on me. I was deeply committed to making the company a success. During the first few years, I worked fourteen-hour days growing the business, forming relationships throughout the city, and bringing in clients. It was not uncommon for me to put on a uniform and pull guard duty at a job site when we were short-staffed. I didn't mind the hard work and grueling schedule, because the business was my baby. I was in charge. At GM I might have been a supervisor, but here, my old entrepreneurial skills dating back to my youth had room and reason to bud on a bigger scale. Now, I was birthing something from scratch, something to call my own. And like any caring mother, I gladly sacrificed and did everything in my power to nurture my "brain child," so to speak. This baby business grew very fast. After eight years, it was generating four million dollars in revenue.

"Sis, you were born for this," observed my brother one day, as we talked about business strategies. You just have this uncanny ability to get clients. I think it's a gift, you know, to be able to connect, win people over and form relationships like you do, in any social circle. Yeah Sis, that's a gift,"

Well, it seems I was not as skilled in picking the right business partner. As our business thrived, the partnership started to crack under the weight of mistrust, fuss over revenue-sharing, and legal matters. I felt used and utterly betrayed by my partner, and a nasty blow-up ensued right before Christmas of 2000. For me, it was the last straw. The partnership had been fractured beyond repair. Right then and there, my mind was made up to sever ties. I wanted nothing more to do with my business partner at the time, nor the business. So I did what shocked most people.

"What do you mean you're going to just walk away?" a trusted, longtime friend shouted over the phone in disbelief.

"Have you lost your mind, Mary Parker? You built that business!"

"Girl, I just can't deal with it any more, the strain is killing me,"

So I walked away from my multi-million dollar security firm and looked back only to reflect on the harsh lessons learned.

In retrospect, my advice to potential business owners is to take the needed time to vet business partners and perform thorough due diligence. In my case, the moment things began to spiral out of control, it hit me we did not have operating agreements in place. In fact, we had not even executed a legal partnership deal, nor did we set processes for how we'd share profit or settle disputes. There was absolutely nothing in writing. The multi-million dollar business had been foolishly built on trust, alone. It was a bitter and costly lesson to learn. When you start a business with friends, family members of anybody for that matter, never take someone's word without also getting it in writing.

When you're just starting out and the business is not making money, it doesn't matter who owns the company, partners are on the same level. Be mindful that the business will start to generate a profit and the decision-making process then changes. This is where things can get ugly, even nasty if there is ever a business dispute. This is why it's critical that you have your operating agreement in place.

Unfortunately, in my case, I was the trusting, weaker partner, not knowing what I did not know.

My role in the company was not just to serve as President but to put on a guard uniform whenever someone didn't show up for work. Such wasn't the case for my business partner. He was still working in Corporate America and still had an established income. My income was contingent upon his support as well as what, if anything, the company could pay me. The painful truth was that my partner held all of the cards, and I was losing. You're losing when you don't have those clear expectations spelled out in an agreement that is signed by you and your partner. But what's even more important is that all agreements and specification documents should be reviewed by two separate attorneys. That's if you want to protect yourself. There is no two-for-one deals in business. Always look out for number one—you.

Sometimes we go into business not realizing that we have a personal need for legal protection. A mistake some business partners make is that everything they do in the business is done as a corporation, meaning done to protect the corporation, not themselves. This is dangerous. My partner and I did have a corporate attorney for our business. What I learned was that I needed a legal attorney for myself, which was crucial. Without my own legal representation, I was out in the cold in the event something happened. And unfortunately, it did.

Women especially need to be careful. Generally, women are more prone to trust, which can set us up for failure. Make your most earnest plea before any judge and they will tell you, "Ignorance of the law is no defense." Saying, *Oh well, I thought...* doesn't hold water in a court of law. The good thing is there are laws established to protect us. We have to implement that protection by doing the things required on the front side. The golden rule is to have everything you are agreeing to in writing. Never leave your signed agreement at the office. Take it home or keep it off site in a safe place. Be sure to make a copy of your stock ledger as well as every share of the stock early in a relationship. Believe it or not, it's very easy for things to be tampered with, more so today than it was with me fifteen years ago. You could be under the impression that you own fifty percent of the company only to later learn that the numbers were changed without your knowledge. Another word of caution is that if you can't verify your claim, it's your loss. Taken together, it's best to have your own personal business file off site at a secure location while working within any partnership. The partnership could be with family, spouse, or friend, it makes no difference. Leave nothing to chance. Again, get all agreements in writing. It takes emotion out of things, and it protects you down the road.

Unfortunately, in business, women often think with their heart. This has its warm virtues and advantages, but it can also burn them in business. I've learned the hard way. Granted, some people accuse me of not showing compassion, but the truth is I am very compassionate. I am also a woman who's been scorned, who's been deceived, who's been betrayed, and who has lost everything as a result of taking my business partner at his word. When it was clear that the differences between us were irreconcilable, I left the company. Since we had nothing in writing, it could have turned into a nasty knock-down drag-out sort of fight. This was something I did not want. So walking away from my four million-dollar company was the best solution.

I remember talking to my brother Rick, and through my bitter tears and a broken heart, declared that I was at the end of my rope.

"I'm done. This is the last straw. *Come pick me up,"* I admitted.

Life's experiences had taught me that a setback is a setup for a comeback. I had walked that road before in Michigan. Getting demoted from Security Director was a painful blow for a high achiever like me. Ironically, it's what shifted my mindset. It got me angry enough to seriously consider stepping out on my own and starting my own security company.

Success Magazine publisher Darren Hardy once said, "Your adversities are your biggest advantage." Adversities can push us to work harder, try daring and new ideas, be more creative, or make our better best. History is filled with rich character profiles of ordinary people doing extraordinary things after they had flopped, failed, been rejected, or were counted out. Look at Thomas Edison, whose teachers told him he was too stupid to learn anything. The nineteenth century inventor is best known, among others things, for inventing the light bulb. But it took him more than a thousand failed attempts to finally get it right. Most of the bright ideas that have changed the world were conceived by people who used failure as a catalyst to succeed.

Yes, some friends thought I had lost my mind because I had walked away from a profitable business. They would repeatedly ask, *"How could you just give up your four -million dollar business, especially with all the years of sweat equity invested?"* They couldn't get past the idea of losing so much money. My first answer to them was philosophical. *Those who know how to make money can lose it all, for they can use their knowledge to make it all back again.* Clients and other colleagues expected my return in the security industry. As the saying goes, it's the "know how" that's the treasure. My second answer called on a higher power for comfort and assurance. I believed that because it was God who conceived within me the idea for a security company, surely He could help me birth another baby. And that's exactly what He would later do.

In the meantime, however, I no longer had a security business, and was broke. Even the car I drove belonged to the company, so that went too.

DIVINE INTERVENTION

Not long after that dreadful day, Rick had an unplanned conversation with the Chief of Security at Clark Atlanta University, A.J. White. Rick had worked there as dean for student affairs. With the exception of usual pleasantries, Rick said he and the chief had never engaged in conversation. But this time, for no apparent reason, they talked like old friends. Rick is still convinced it was the Spirit of God who led him to ask the chief if he knew of anyone with a security company that needed assistance.

"I've got my own security company," Chief White replied.

Thinking that he might have heard the man wrong, Rick asked him to repeat his statement.

Again, the chief answered, "I have my own security company."

Rick enthusiastically vouched for me, citing all of my qualifications, skills, and accomplishments, including the fact that I had started my own company but had to walk away unexpectedly. I'm pretty certain that there was an expanded conversation of some sort, but most importantly, my destiny was being worked out behind closed doors, without my knowledge. This is a true manifestation of divine intervention. Who would have known that out of all the industries, the chief would have started his own security company? But just like that, divine intervention played a pivotal part in my life, at the appointed time.

I still had the loyalty and support of several clients from my previous business. But to keep them, I desperately needed a license. The earliest scheduled license testing was months away. I needed a miracle badly, and God responded to my need. So, what are the odds of someone securing a security license, holding on to it for years, and showing up in my life at the precise moment it was needed? That had the Divine's fingerprint all over it.

Many a business deal have been secured at Atlanta's historic Pascal's Restaurant. And that's where the security chief, Rick, and I sealed a deal.

"Ok Mary, so let's all understand this. I give you control of my company, with full use of my license until you get your own."

"That's right, chief" I affirmed. "And in exchange, you will retain twenty percent ownership and partnership profits over the next five years" "OK, I think we got ourselves a deal," the chief said, with satisfaction.

And this is how ALL(n)1 Security was born. The name suggests full security service. But I was not thinking that far ahead when I came up with the name. The "ALL(n)1" title represents the Trinity— Father, Son, and Holy Spirit. It's a testament to God being my security and protector through the ups and downs of my growth process and life journey.

My fledging company started as a physical security business, meaning that the services consisted of having guards in uniforms protecting buildings, people, and assets from potential theft, plain and simple. Initially, I had no grand business plan or strategic vision. Things seem to easily fall into place, so much so that my brother Rick dubbed me the "haphazard genius." He would often say that I "happen upon" amazing business opportunities by chance or divine favor. Now, this might be true. But I am wise enough to know what to do with opportunities when they show up. Well before the deal was cut, I was already taking charge, working as though my new security company was up and running. In fact, I had secured a contract for service before I even got the license. Of the list of former loyal clients I had invited to join me at ALL(n)1, all but one did. Chastain Park was among the first to do so, based solely on my longstanding relationship with the park director, Rudy Schlegal. This landed us a $300,000 contract to secure the park for the summer months.

But our first new job as ALL(n)1 Security was a sweet deal with The Fox Theatre. We were hired to provide security at an Erykah Badu concert in 2001. Relying on ties I had with a friend landed ALL(n)1 Security its first gig. That night, we cleared $4,700. It was enough to pay my security guards and stash away some cash for several months of rent. This lucrative deal took place less than three months after the business had gone into operation.

As the months and years passed, ALL(n)1 Security flourished. Today, it is now a multi-million dollar business that provides employment for nearly three hundred people. Its beginning is as humble as my sharecropping roots in rural Mississippi. My baby brother Rick was a silent partner, handling payroll and the company's financial dealings away from the office. It would be five or six years before he came on board full time. In the meantime, I ran the company as the majority shareholder and became the public face of ALL(n)1 Security.

It was if we had the golden touch. In the first year, we landed more than $300,000 in contracts. In our second year, the company hauled in more than $700,000 in revenue. It wasn't long before the news media came knocking, and that public face and my story were plastered on the covers of local magazines and on television. The business was featured as the female-run business making fast tracks in a highly competitive male-dominated industry. We were dubbed one of Atlanta's small business success stories. All of this free publicity helped to seal ALL(n)1's reputation as I continued to secure deals with clients. And this was my specialty.

A top executive for a major Atlanta Gas company had just given a speech at a forum, and was leaving the conference room in a hurry. I only had a few seconds to intercept his stride and stop him in the hallway. All I needed was a few minutes to make my pitch. Not wanting to waste the gentleman's time, I complimented his speech and got straight to the point.

"Yes, please allow me to show you how ALL(n)1 Security will change the way you look at off duty law enforcement officers. We are a one stop, one contact, one contract solutions provider."

What amounted to a ten-minute conversation with a complete stranger eventually turned into a 3 million dollar business contract—Yes, 3 million dollars! Our brief exchange so impressed the executive that it led to a phone call. In the end, the call yielded an $800,000 security contract within a year. Then within three years it grew to 3 million! How did this happen? It took being bold, affable, determined, and skilled in building meaningful relationships.

Ask yourself, how bold and fearless are you in securing what you want or need for your business growth? What's your risk tolerance? Are you confident and determined enough to throw caution to the wind and create ways to meet that one client who could catapult your business to the next level?

Be Bold. You can't be afraid to go after what you want in business or in life.

Be Affable. Nothing breaks down the walls of resistance more rapidly than a smile and a friendly spirit.

Be Determined. Life's greatest successes were born out of failures, setbacks and rejections. The winning edge has always been the will to try and try again.

Build Relationships. No business can survive without relationships. It's the key to unlocking your customers' needs and desires.

It was relationship with our clients in the field that exposed me to traffic control as another avenue to generate business. Before then, I never knew it existed. Traffic control is when off-duty police officers direct traffic in a temporary construction work zone while utility companies are performing repairs and service. If a gas line broke or needed repair, Atlanta Gas Light would send out a crew and would need an officer to direct traffic around the work zone. With this new endeavor we quickly expanded ALL(n)1 and added a traffic control unit to our operation.

Then one day while our guys were out directing traffic, my client asked a question that opened another door of opportunity.

"So Miss Parker, since your crew is already out here, can they install the traffic control equipment? We might as well give you that contract too, if you can do the job,"

"Of course we can do it, I assured quite confidently, even though I had absolutely no idea what it entailed.

Our security company had no experience or background in setting up on-site equipment. But I was astute enough of a businessperson to never say no to a business expansion opportunity just because I didn't necessarily possess the expertise. A *Chick in Charge* knows that everything you need to learn is locked in a book or can be found somewhere Online. Given this, Rick and I took a few courses, became certified, and allowed on-the-job training to do the rest. Before long, we were experts not only in traffic control, but we had acquired the engineering knowledge to provide the specialized work zone equipment required to safeguard a traffic site. This meant more work and more revenue.

In early 2000, ALL(n)1 morphed again. This time, we added the most profitable component to the business—technology enterprise. Installing closed-circuit TVs for our commercial clients offered them a more sophisticated layer of protection and accountability. If something should happen in a parking lot or at night the cameras capture and store everything on the premises. Since technology remains a viable business requirement, Rick, who now serves as company president, spearheaded plans to have up to sixty-percent of ALL(n)1 Security services coming from the technology sector over a five-year period. Talk about business strategy and planning!

CHAPTER SIX

Position Yourself for Profit

Every great dream begins with a dreamer. Always remember, you have within you the strength, the patience, and the passion to reach for the stars to change the world.
Harriet Tubman

ONE OF THE HARDEST THINGS FOR BUSINESS OWNERS TO DO IS TO admit internal weakness. Tougher still, is to then commit to change what's not working in their company. It's easy to get entrenched in a company culture of, "doing it this way because that's the way we've always done it." But this stubborn philosophy has bankrupted many businesses, some of whom were generating millions, even billions of dollars a year.

Who remembers Circuit City? At the turn of the twenty-first century, Circuit City was the second largest appliance retailer in the country. It boasted twelve billion dollars in sales revenue, and yet just eight years later, in 2008, the firm that pioneered the big box electronics concept went bankrupt. How is that possible? How can a business with billions of dollars in revenue collapse and die?

Are there subtle warning or failure signs that small businesses need to watch for? A careful study of why that giant retailer fell reveals unique lessons every entrepreneur or small business owner can learn from.

CIRCUIT CITY'S SHORT CIRCUIT

Circuit City started as a small mom and pop store in Richmond, Virginia in 1949. Alan Wurtzel's father founded the business. He said of his dad, "The day he opened the store, he thought it would be a billion-dollar company." Isn't that the wild and wonderful ambition of so many entrepreneurs? We start out with a ready desire to dominate our market and conquer the world.

During its sixty year growth, Circuit City became a household name. It amassed a workforce that employed more than forty thousand people. At its peak, fifteen hundred Circuit City superstores dotted the landscape across the U.S. and Canada. It became a Wall Street darling and a magnet for eager investors. So how did this mother of electronic supercenters short circuit itself?

Well before Circuit City began to crumble, Alan Wurtzel had relinquished the helm as company CEO. He was among the mourners the day a U.S. Bankruptcy judge finally pulled the plug on Circuit City. He wanted answers as to why the family business suffered such a dreadful death. Wurtzel's book, *Good to Great to Gone: The Sixty Year Rise and Fall of Circuit City*, is the result of his personal investigation and painstaking search for what went wrong. He concluded that the company's culture was slow to identify radical industry change and even slower to respond.

"Circuit City's lifespan proves that businesses have to fight hard every day." Wurtzel also noted that because the world is always changing, business owners can't rely on past accomplishments. As we can see, the celebrated company became a behemoth too slow to keep up with rapidly shifting consumer habits. It wasn't nimble enough to adjust when innovative competitors such as Best Buy began moving in on its market share, and by the time executives finally tried to change the culture, it was too late. When the financial crisis hit in 2007, Circuit City's creditors hurriedly backed away. The once rock-solid company simply did not have enough operating capital to offset a severe credit-freeze.

Here's a lesson any thoughtful entrepreneur can learn from Circuit City's shortfall and subsequent collapse, and it is to pay attention to industry trends, be ready to shift with the changing times, and be quick to fix what does not work.

Take Charge of Your Destiny

Fixing what wasn't working at ALL(n)1 Security was tough. By all appearances, we were a very successful company. In 2001, ALL(n)1 started out as a physical security firm. We provided guards to secure buildings. We safeguarded a wide range of special events, including concerts, trade shows and sporting events, and we also offered executive protection for celebrities.

Contrary to typical small business start-ups, ALL(n)1 started out debt-free. We did not qualify for a line of credit from the bank. As a silent partner, my brother Rick advanced payroll for the first year. My first contract generated enough revenue to pay off operating expenses and even left a tidy profit. So the company started making money right on the launching pad and then took off like a rocket. But we had no structure, no strategy, not even a business plan.

One thing I did have was a strong work ethic, thanks to my upbringing on that Mississippi sharecropping farm. So I worked myself close to the brink of a physical and mental breakdown to secure a portfolio of impressive clients. And in just three years, my new security business was clearing almost one million dollars. Yes, the company was making money providing top notch security service to our clients. But there was a problem. Analytically, we did not know how we were making money or what it was costing us. One day I called up my account to help me calculate the cost of goods sold and was surprised by what was told to me.

"Well, Mary, we can't calculate that cost because you sell a service not a product."

"Yeah, so…but it's costing us to run the service, so how much is it costing us? I responded. I knew there had to be an associated cost, and I was not willing to walk away without a monetary figure.

"Well, we can't come up with cost of service," the accountant conveyed one last time.

I later fired that accountant. While it was true that we were generating lucrative revenue, we needed to become experts on our numbers. A business cannot secure long-term success if it doesn't know bottom line costs. In other words, what it costs to deliver a product or service. Like me, many entrepreneurs had hung out their shingle and lured in customers with having absolutely no clue what their billable or overhead rates are. For instance, I pay a worker ten dollars an hour to guard a business. And I bill my client, the business owner, eighteen dollars an hour for the service. The eight-dollar spread might seem like a profit. But it's just revenue. Profit is what's left over, once all expenses are paid. That eight dollar difference might not be enough to cover my overhead costs, let alone make me a true profit.

So if I don't know what it costs me to pay that person ten dollars an hour, I might end up taking a loss and not making a profit. I have to factor in things such as workers compensation, uniform costs, the cost of my office rental space, and the cost to pay my accountant. All that must be factored into a formula. At ALL(n)1, we were getting a steady flow of revenue from clients who bought our service. And even though the company looked successful on paper, I had no idea what it was costing us to make money. At times, it was quite frustrating.

As CEO and president of ALL(n)1, I was simply doing what I knew to do to keep the business operational. But there was no system or process in place to track, quantify, or even sustain our rapid growth. To the outside world, ALL(n)1 was thriving. But privately, it felt like a house of cards. I feared one wrong move and the company would collapse. I was flying by the seat of my pants while managing to make money. No wonder my brother Rick called me a haphazard genius. But increasingly, I felt more like haphazard fool trying desperately to juggle my private struggles and ALL(n)1's public image of unprecedented success. At time, I felt as though I was only keeping up appearances, and that I was a fraud waiting to be exposed. *What would people think if they only knew I was drowning in my own success?*

In the meantime, ALL(n)1 Security was being hailed as the rising star in the industry. I, again, became a darling in the press with articles and headlines applauding my success. Invitations to speak at conferences as a business expert poured in.

I recall traveling to Savannah, Georgia to speak at an event with my friend, Arthur Bronner. His family owns The Bronner Bros. Enterprise, one of the country's largest private African-American hair and skin care manufacturers. My speech was titled, "The Set Back is a Set Up for the Comeback." It highlighted my journey in business from my first security company "failure" to running a successful and rapidly growing security firm. The irony was lost on everybody else except me.

As I stood there at the podium, an empty, hollow feeling crept over me. My taunting thoughts whispered that my words to the attentive audience were not totally sincere. I felt like I was faking the speech. Because, again, while I looked successful on paper, I didn't feel successful. And my outward appearance of impeccable confidence didn't always hide the internal struggle.

It was Mr. Bronner who took a good look at my countenance after I spoke that day. He waited for the opportune time, and then he took the liberty to share with me what he had observed.

"I see you smiling, Mary, but it's such a sad smile. There is no joy."

I was stunned. He read me like a book. But I was too ashamed to open up and reveal my internal turmoil.

"You are here, my friend, but you are not present," he continued.

What Mr. Bronner had shared felt burdensome to me. It seemed I had become an expert at putting on the face of success.

Mary, it's time to take off the mask and change what isn't working, I admitted to myself that very moment. It was time to become transparent. I had to admit that, while I may be the *Chick in Charge*, I was not super woman. I needed help making sense of my growing business. So I let out a desperate, heart-felt cry to God for help. And his answer came swiftly.

Soon after my plea for divine intervention, a unique opportunity showed up for me to join an elite mastermind club of millionaire CEO's. But I shrunk back. *"Who am I to think I could be counted as a bona fide member of such a prestigious group?*

With such negative thinking and internal fear, I flatly turned down the first invitation to join. The internal critic persisted. *You don't know enough to be with all those CEOs.* I had to admit that feared if I joined, these people would discover that I really didn't have it all together. So I convinced myself to stay back, keep hiding, and keep doing business the way I was doing it, with the claim that no one had to know about my inner struggles.

How many small businesses die on the vine, not solely because of lack of funds but because their owners became overwhelmed and lost their passion? I'd venture to say quite a few. Some entrepreneurs start off with a firm idea of how their business will take shape and run. However, when challenges arise, they refuse to be flexible and make the necessary adjustments to adapt to change. And a bankrupt Circuit City is evidence that a business doesn't have to be a struggling start-up to fall into this trap.

Sometimes, businesses get stuck at a certain level of success. They hit a concrete ceiling and isolate themselves instead of reaching out for help. That's a blueprint for business failure. There are mentors, business coaches, and even some free government programs designed to help struggling small businesses retool or even reinvent themselves. But like me at the time, so many business owners are unwilling to admit they are in trouble and need help.

Lucky for me, the Millionaire CEO Mastermind group came after me again the following year. Thankfully, this time, I said yes. By then, ALL(n)1 had grown to more than a million dollars in annual revenue, and I still did not know how we were doing it. So I was ready for help, even though it meant potentially exposing my hairline fractures, those business weaknesses that, if not dealt with, would hurt my growth and inevitably confine me to a level of small scale success. I kept remembering what God had revealed to me about my business, and there was nothing small scale or limiting about that vision. I knew that to take ALL(n)1 Security to a place of exponential, multi-million dollar growth, I had to turbo-charge. As CEO, I had to shift to a multi-million dollar, knowledge-based mindset.

Mind you, I had always been anxious to learn anything and everything about my industry. I had taken every possible advanced, certified or specialized training course, at great financial cost to me. I was proactive in keeping my business relevant, competitive and cutting-edge. While all that was good, something was still missing. But I found the missing link when I joined the Millionaire Mastermind Group. To quantum leap my company, I had to mingle with minds far above my current level of thinking. Hitching my rising star to the millionaire mastermind partners was one of the best business decisions I have ever made. And as I would later discover, it would dramatically shift the trajectory of my business and my life.

One of the first things I did after joining was become brutally honest with myself about my feelings, inadequacies, and fears. I shared my concerns with Rita, the woman who ran the mastermind program.

"Let's get a few things clear. I need to learn how to be the real me. I need to be transparent, even if it is going to hurt me, initially."

"True," Rita agreed.

"But my dilemma is that it's gonna hurt the clients I represent, because people won't believe in me anymore. They are going to think that I have been a lie."

Rita was silent. She just stared at me, until I confessed my truth—*I had just been managing the business with what I knew to do.*

"I can help you," Rita replied confidently.

The group was comprised of experts in various areas of business. Everything I needed to shift my company to the multi-million dollar level, someone in this elite group could offer specialized knowledge and support. We became each other's advisors. One company concentrated on training people in sales, another specialized in financial matters, and others brought their unique brand of expertise to the table. At first I was intimidated, again thinking members were going to laugh at my measly one million-dollar business portfolio. But I went in and bore all to them. I was totally transparent. I admitted my struggles and weaknesses, even my fears. What I received in return was priceless council on effective collaboration, strategic partnerships, and a kinship with entrepreneurs who were big thinkers and high performers. Like that giddy, child back in Horse Penn, eager to ask one hundred and one questions, I picked their brains clean. I learned to diagnose the health of my business and administer the proper treatment.

They say birds of a feather flock together. If you want to aim high in life, track down the soaring eagles in your industry. Learn and adapt their ways. You'll notice their flight patterns are steady and deliberate. After flying with my mastermind eagles, I discovered that I needed to establish an advisory board for my business and a board of directors. I needed to create a strong and savvy support team.

For two and a half years I soared with these millionaire master-minds. I gobbled up every specialized industry training course and became certified in every educational program suggested. I made sure no one around me knew more about my business than I did. This allowed me to continue to soar. In the early 2000's, I enrolled in the Tuck Executive Leadership Training at Dartmouth College. There, I learned I had to incorporate thirty-three business strategies and refine my business operation. According to Dartmouth, it was a must if I was to "survive, prosper, and grow to scale."

So intense was my hunger to develop a superior security busi-ness, in just eighteen months I had fully implemented thirty of the thirty three strategies in my company. They included developing a marketing strategy, creating and implementing an in house accounting system, and developing banking and legal relationships. Together, these gave me the creative acumen to build a strong and stable business foundation.

Yes! Finally, I had learned how to implement systems and processes, critical infrastructures necessary for any business to be high performing and thrive in a competitive environment.

Not long after my schooling, these new measures proved their value in a moment of crisis. One Friday, after we had paid our employees, we quickly discovered that payroll funds were short. Money to cover the shortfall wouldn't get to the bank in time to avert a financial nightmare. I quickly called my banker and explained to him the situation. And since we had developed a trusted relationship, my word alone was good enough for him to clear the incoming payroll checks until the funds caught up several days later.

As you can see, it's critical to be passionate about your business. It's one key prerequisite to staying the course when the ride to success gets bumpy. You also have to be profoundly knowledgeable of your product or services. Understanding your finances is what's most critical to business survival and sustained success.

To hit on all cylinders I had to change and admit my company's internal weakness. It could no longer be business as usual. Investing in my personal growth at a higher level was a must. The Dartmouth business training along with the Millionaire CEO Mastermind group cost me more than thirty-two thousand dollars. That training exposed me to strategies that catapulted ALL(n)1 to another stratosphere and transformed the way we do business. Now we have the right people on our team. We have clearly defined processes and procedures and effective systems in place to execute those processes. Without these components a company can get stuck and won't grow. Moreover, without these components, you may be running a hobby not a business.

CHAPTER SEVEN
Give What You've Been Given

The delicate balance of mentoring someone is not creating them in your own image, but giving them the opportunity to create themselves.
Steven Spielberg

WORLD-RENOWNED ENTREPRENEUR AND PHILANTHROPIST MARY Kay Ash once said, "The fun thing about getting older is finding younger people to mentor." As I get older, I, too, am finding pleasure in pouring into young business owners eager to learn.

Getting older also gives me reason to pause, to look back on my mentors from whose well of wisdom I drank. I was born thirsty for purpose and significance. So whatever my trusted advisors suggested, I did. Some gave generously of their time and their council. Others offered a road map with clear directives that fed my drive to achieve big things. These mentors helped shape my business philosophy and ultimately, helped cement my success.

A MENTOR'S TOUCH

No one did that more directly than my dear and long-time friend, George Logan. He's been my business confidante and sounding board for more than twenty-five years. It was George who exposed me to a world I had no idea existed in the security industry, a world of security executives who worked for top corporations and made six figure salaries doing it. In this world, George was called the Godfather of black security executives. This was because he lent his time to mentor the handful of African Americans who had made it to the upper echelon of the security industry. So he was well respected.

George held a high-level position as the World-Wide Director of Security for General Mills, a food company based in Minneapolis. Among other things, he traveled the world protecting celebrities such as basketball great Michael Jordan, pro-football star Walter Payton, and Olympic gold medalist Bruce Jenner. All three top athletes, at different times, were spokesmen for Wheaties, a General Mills breakfast cereal. And each traveled extensively to promote the popular brand.

I met George in September of 1990. He was what I called, "a strong black brother." He had clout and character, and he cared deeply for those mentees he gathered around him. George was one of the six founding members the IOBSE, which is the acronym that stands for the International Organization of Black Security Executives. The organization was founded in 1986 as a result of the founders being troubled that so few people of color were in the security industry, much less worked as top executives, in management, or technical positions. The goal was to use the organization to mentor college level young people on how to break into security and to share the members' vast experiences with the students. Organization members visited historically black colleges and targeted students in criminal justice programs, and they shared one clear message—that there is more to security than being police officers or parole officers, or anything connected with the court system. There exists this little known, yet more lucrative industry to be considered.

Most of the young people had never heard of security as a profession. They only knew about security guards and security personnel who worked in stores to catch shoplifters. But George and his colleagues were all senior-level security executives at various corporations such as General Mills and Mobile Oil. IOBSE felt few people of color gravitated to these positions because they were unaware that such an industry existed. In fact, even I had never heard of a profession outside the guard ranks in security. So when I attended my first IOBSE meeting, I was in both shock and awe learning of the growth possibilities for me as a fledging entrepreneur.

By 1994, I became one of George's mentees. Like a dry sponge, I soaked up every bit of information he shared, and then I moved quickly to apply it in my business. Since my company supplied security guards to firms like the ones IOBSE members worked for, George introduced me to key industry people who could use my services. He assisted me in presenting my company to General Mills. He introduced me to key players and decision makers for security across the corporate America spectrum.

Having a well-respected, high-level executive like George recommending me, opened doors and opportunities that, on my own, I would not have even known existed. I made it my business to stay close to George and gleaned all I could about the industry. In fact, I joined the IOBSE and stayed an active member for many years. Doing so gave me access to a treasure trove of knowledge. And the chance to be groomed by the "Godfather" was priceless.

At General Mills, George was the man charged with protecting the company's employees and resources, worldwide. This involved everything from setting up security in various manufacturing plants, to developing and implementing programs to prevent contamination of the product, especially raw ingredients. The company hauled in sugar and flour by the truck load to make cereal. These days, security duties also include being vigilant against potential terrorist threats. So there was always a chance for contamination by disgruntled employees. As Director of Security, George, along with others at General Mills, developed a program for workplace violence that allowed managers in the field to spot troubled employees who might later become violent.

A recipe is treated like gold, which is why companies like General Mills work hard to protect their proprietary or confidential information. George talks of the time someone tried to steal the recipe for Cheerios, the biggest-selling cereal in the world. The conspiracy was actually discovered to be an "inside job." An employee tried to sell the trade secret to the competition, Kellogg's Company. But it didn't work because of security processes in place that were implemented under the direction of General Mills' executive directorship.

Imagine me, peaking into George's world and taking copious notes on how to run the security operation for a multi-billion dollar company. And I did just that!

George's rise to his high-level post in the security industry grew from humble beginnings. In fact, it turns out that my mentor and I had a lot in common. I grew up a sharecropper's daughter in rural Mississippi; he was raised by working class parents in the inner city of Philadelphia. He had nine siblings and was next to the oldest. I, too, was the second born of nine children. We also shared a childhood of honest, hard work, and integrity. And integrity has been a personal philosophy George is well known for. He taught me the importance of having integrity in the security industry. He would sometimes say, "Mary, security represents integrity. It represents honesty. It represents being able to communicate. It represents earning the respect of others, because if they don't respect you, they will cut your legs off."

George also taught me the importance of developing strong business relationships on a personal level, beyond the surface. This way, genuine friendships are formed. So when "push comes to shove" you always have someone you can depend on, someone you can trust.

George taught me about family values. He had the most beautiful wife and two lovely children. Occasionally, when I visited them, I'd notice the way that he treated his wife, so gently and with so much love. George also took pride in his bedrock principles, one of which was honesty. George not only told me these things, he showed me these things. I witnessed many instances of his integrity, honesty, and loyalty, and I will briefly share one memorable incident with you. I had gone shopping with George and his family when they visited Atlanta during the 1996 Summer Olympics. His daughter tried to exchange a Louis Vuitton bag at a different store than where she purchased it. But George was not having it.

"Did you buy this bag from this Louis Vuitton store?" he questioned his daughter, suspecting she was engaging in a deceptive practice.

When his daughter hesitated to give him an honest answer, George looked her firmly in the eyes and gave her a profound lecture on integrity.

"It's the integrity. If you didn't buy it from them, you cannot return it to them. You return it where you bought it, and let them return it, if that's their policy. But you will not come in here to return this purse as though you bought it from them."

Someone else privy to that conversation might have thought George was a bit overzealous. But that's how meticulous he was about his values, and he was just as zealous about having his children adopt them as well.

George was very wise with his spending, and he made sure that he took his family on the best vacations. His appetite for Broadway shows in New York and trips to Paris, Brazil, Australia, and London gave me a hunger to spread my wings as well. Now it's nothing for me to hop on a plane and go enjoy certain comforts of life.

"Too many people go to work for everybody else. When you go to work every day, Mary, you've got to have yourself and your family in mind as well. Every day I was planning how much money I needed to save, what we would do with the money, and how much I wanted to set up for my children," George said during one of our conversations. And I have never forgotten this golden nugget.

George understood financial management very early in life. He bought stocks in all the companies he had worked with—including Levi Strauss and General Mills. Wherever he worked he bought the maximum amount of stocks, and he never touched his investments. He also took advantage of the IRAs, Roth accounts, everything that he could do to defer his taxes. It is no question that George retired very comfortably.

George had a lot to offer when it came to being business savvy. He was a man who took full charge of his life by deliberately plotting the course to success. And as he shared his journey, I took copious notes. The more I asked, the more he gave. The more he gave, the more I implemented in my own life. With George Logan on my team, I was well on my way to being "The *Chick in Charge*" of my finances.

I followed George's advice on investing in insurances—term versus whole life— annuities, and stock options, how to purchase stock, the types of things to look for, and irrevocable living trusts. These are things I had either never heard of before or gave much attention. My mentor taught me the wisdom of having a mixed or very diverse portfolio, and not to put a lot of emphasis on liquid or on cash. Some people may say cash is king. But George advised me to keep cash limited and keep resources and investments at a maximum.

Four decades before, I had watched, with great fascination, how Uncle T carefully selected the ingredients to mix up his batch of bootleg liquor. Now, I was just as taken in by every step my mentor meted out on how to brew up sustainable financial success. And it sobered me up to a world of wealthy possibilities I had never known before. George Logan taught me how to take charge of my finances in a fashion that would quantum-leap my net worth. It would also shift the very foundation of my family tree.

You can get up close and personal with a mentor like George Logan. And I did. But other mentors had no idea I was learning from them, grazing in their garden from a distance. These are people you notice, admire, and model from a far. This is how my relationship with Xernona Clayton started. She is the classy, take-charge business woman who has inspired me most.

This civil rights activist and broadcasting executive often jokes about always being the smallest person in the room. She stands just above four feet tall. But what Ms. Clayton lacks in physical stature she makes up for with her towering influence and graceful aura that consume any room she enters. Mention the 1960's Civil Rights Movement and Ms. Clayton's name is etched in between the lines of the conversation. She never marched in public, afraid of getting arrested. But in private, Xernona moved mountains and dismantled stubborn racial barriers with her charm and tactical skills. She was a subtle but strategic game-changer.

In 1968, Atlanta woke up to stunning news headlines screaming, Xernona Clayton, 'The Dragon Slayer." Somehow, Ms. Clayton had quietly befriended the Grand Dragon of the Georgia Ku Klux Klan. Over time, she had convinced him to denounce the Klan. Calvin Craig later resigned his position. He and Ms. Clayton then became the strangest of odd couples. They traveled together, holding joint interviews on the fight for integration in the South. Ms. Clayton knew how to gracefully disarm her adversaries, and at the same time, have them "eating out of her hands," as she puts it.

Working in a male-dominated industry, I've learned to do just that. I am usually the only woman and the only person of color at the table. Like Ms. Clayton, I've had to use charm and witty intelligence to "sooth the savage beasts" who at times tried to intimidate or steam roll me.

Ms. Clayton worked under-cover for the National Urban League to root out entrenched racial discrimination in companies. She corralled black doctors to push for desegregation at all Atlanta hospitals, and it happened. She worked tirelessly to improve the quality of desegregated neighborhoods through a federally funded program. She was "a mover and a shaker." Ms. Clayton was one of the "quiet powers" and stable pillars in Dr. Martin Luther King Junior's inner circle. She organized events for the Southern Christian Leadership, helped plan marches, and arranged King's schedule. It was Ms. Clayton who drove the civil rights leader to the Atlanta airport on the fateful trip to Memphis where he was assassinated. It was this close family friend whom Coretta Scott King entrusted to comfort the four King children as she hurried off to face the maddening aftermath of her Dr. King's death.

This comforter-in-charge also blazed a trail as a media pioneer. Ms. Clayton was the first African-American woman in the south to host her own prime time TV show. Just imagine how that must of delighted little black girls glued to the tube, giddily watching someone who looked like them. Ms. Clayton later worked for Turner Broadcasting, rising to the top to become as Vice President of Public Affairs. She used her position and her close friendship with Ted Turner to improve the company's ethnic and racial culture.

Today, most people know Ms. Clayton as the founder of the prestigious Trumpet Awards. Every year, it honors outstanding black achievement and civil right advocates. Ms. Clayton's Trumpet Award Foundation has raised more than four million dollars in student scholarship funds. Now at 85 years old, she is still as timeless and faithful as the sun and still sits at the helm of her beloved foundation. The cities of Atlanta and her hometown of Muskogee, Oklahoma have both celebrated Ms. Clayton as a living legend, naming streets in her honor.

When this living legend personally contacted me in the summer of 2010, you should understand why my heart skipped a beat or two. The woman I so admired from afar had been admiring me from a distance. Having read a newspaper article chronicling the rapid success of my security business, she called and invited me to receive her High Heels Award. The award is an impressive tribute to women who are in high positions or own their own companies. At our first face-to-face meeting, I left as though I had immediately connected with a warm, kindred spirit.

Ms. Clayton is regarded as the living example of how to "do things right and do things well," which is her mantra. True to my childhood habit, I noticed everything she did. I paid particular attention to how Ms. Clayton attracted people to her circle and shared information. She made it her business to elevate or cast light on quiet, unsung heroes or luminaries who otherwise would go unnoticed. She loved to showcase business or community talent who tend to be busy making their mark while flying under radar.

She went to Africa and opened a school for young people there. Through her foundation, she awards scholarships to deserving individuals every year. And for years now, even as a very successful business owner, I privately watched Ms. Clayton and modeled some of her business methods. I still marvel at Xernona Clayton's charisma, elegance, and the grace in which she moves. She is definitely a golden wonder and stands in a space all by herself. She may never know how the broad reach of her influence has helped to reshape my resolve to touch lives and leave my own legacy.

Chapter Eight

Follow Your Spiritual Compass

With God all thigs are possible...
Matthew 19:26

M Y COUSIN BETTY AND I WERE BAPTIZED IN A RIVER OUTSIDE OUR little country church in Denton Town, not far from Horse Pen. I was eight years old at the time. Betty was scared because the make-shift baptismal pool contained frogs and snakes. It did not bother me a bit since very little scared me. I remembered how I felt after Reverend T.J. Giles dunked me in the water. The baptism made me feel safe and protected, as though I had some sort of encounter with God. It took me a while to embrace my spiritual calling, and twenty years would pass after being baptized before it was clear that God had chosen me. My calling was to change the trajectory of my life and also to change my small corner of the business world for Christ. Before this Christian conversion, I simply wanted to be a bad girl. In fact, I tried hard to become a member of the bad girls' club.

PUTTING GOD FIRST

During my days at General Motors, my girlfriend and I loved to attend exclusive private parties. At some of the parties, people drank heavily, and some brothers from out of town would come in strutting their furs and fine threads. Drugs of all sorts were strewn out in plain view, plenty and readily available. My friend and I just wanted to be a part of the "bling-bling" and night life, and truly did not know of the apparent risk and dangers associated with these events. But it seemed that every time I found myself in these environments, something unsettling inside me would say, *leave*. And on at least two occasions, my girlfriend and I left a party only to be met by police at the bottom of the steps or right before the police descended on the premises. On many occasions, the police would go inside, raid it, and arrest people. But somehow we never got arrested.

Things became even worse when I moved to Chicago. Some friends were becoming crack addicts, others got killed, and some went to jail. In witnessing all of this, I still was trying to be a bad girl. The driving force that did not allow me to cross the line was the risk of disappointing my family again. Getting pregnant in high school was a cake walk compared to becoming a crack addict, getting murdered, or going to prison. Also, as a single mom, being available to my daughter was more important than succeeding as a bad girl.

FAITH AND BUSINESS

I don't think we Christian business owners share our testimonies and our core beliefs often enough. I know God allowed me to see the suffering, seedy side of life for a reason. He permitted me to be exposed to those crack houses and juke joints without being sucked in. He knew He could trust me to use the experiences to help deliver others later. In 2008, I was ordained as a minister and became an elder in my church. Seldom will you see me wear the clergy collar, although I do possess the credentials.

Pulpit preaching is necessary. But it's not for me. I was attracted to street ministry—outside the four walls of the church. It's on the street where the lost can be more readily found. This is where I am called to serve, to touch people who may never darken the door of a church, people like my friend Lucy.

I remember Lucy sobbing uncontrollably in my arms. She was a "lady of the night" who was in daily turmoil.

"But Miss Mary, why doesn't he love me?" How come he treats me so bad?" she pleaded, lying in my arms.

"Come now, Lucy, it's going to be okay", I said, searching hard for the right words to re-assure Lucy.

Lucy desperately sought the love of a man who had "pimped" her out for years. She also wanted to make a clean break from this ugly lifestyle, but she was scared. We stood talking on Atlanta's drug-infested Simpson Road where the buckled sidewalk was littered with trash and broken bottles. Many lives here were just as broken. This was the English Avenue community where society's "undesirables" hung out. Twice a week I'd leave my office at ALL(n)1 Security and stalk Simpson Road, looking for the "crack heads," "lowlifes," and prostitutes. These were the clients in my "other business," and as an ordained minister charged with spreading God's love, I offered hope and proof that someone cared enough to meet these "misfits" right where they were. So I'd go looking for the Lucys who needed a shoulder to cry on, a word of encouragement or divine direction on how to escape their daily misery. The way I saw it, I was offering these clients a different type of ALL(n)1 Security—the security that God offers through His love.

Christians are called to be light in a dark world, and that includes in the workplace and in our businesses. We are to influence the current culture. We are called to transform the world system, not conform to its standards. I believe I was predestined to fight my way through racism, sexism, and classism and conquer a white male-dominated industry not just to make money or a name for myself. I am on divine assignment. My business journey to the top of my profession is unequivocal proof of God's faithfulness and miraculous works. It serves as a strategic part of my testimony used to draw others to Christ.

Many Christian business owners struggle with sharing their faith in the marketplace. I don't. My faith is the thread that stitches my business together. Others wonder how they can remain faithful in their Christian walk and run a profitable business. To me, business and faith are not mutually exclusive. My faith does not compete with my business; it complements it. And over the years, this belief has produced much profit for ALL(n)1 Security. I believe business is as much a spiritual journey as it is a natural one. My business values stem from my spiritual values. They do not intersect at some random point, now and then when it's convenient.

There is clear evidence that God provides strategic direction in the world around us. I mean, how many times have we seen this play out on the steps of the nation's Capital in Washington? When a national disaster strikes, our lawmakers set aside their partisan bickering and stand together as one, asking God for help and direction. There was no heated debate about whether it's appropriate to pray or to acknowledge God when Al Qaeda terrorists struck on 9-11 and tried to cripple the country's economy. Sadly, however, once prayers were answered and the crisis passed, God was quickly uninvited from the hallowed halls of Congress. No more public prayer or "kumbaya" moments. That is, until the next national crisis occurs.

Flip over to eleven-fifty-eight in the King James Version of the New Testament, and you'll find nestled in verse forty eight, the secret to my business success—"To whom much is given much is required (expected)." This Bible scripture shapes my personal philosophy and is the foundation on which ALL(n)1 Security was built. Christians are required to perform at a much higher level of excellence than the average entrepreneur. When you apply that scripture to business there is one logical conclusion—God requires us to succeed in our career endeavors. Furthermore, He expects us to excel at the highest level. That's why nothing is impossible for me to achieve once I set my mind to it. God ensures the prosperity of this *Chick in Charge*, because I yield to Him. So the business of ALL(n)1 is really a spiritual journey. My tremendous success is a byproduct of a committed relationship with God and my willingness to obey His instructions on how to properly run the firm. The key to this "business" relationship with the Almighty is prayer.

Why Prayer is Crucial for Business

As an entrepreneur my prayer life is crucial. Every morning, my number one business ritual is not to read the Wall Street Journal or surf the online business of The Atlanta Journal- Constitution. It's to steal away quiet time with God, to pray, meditate and get spiritual guidance before getting swallowed up by another busy day at the office. Allowing the Spirit of God to set the tone renews my mind and gives Him control. Here is the fantastic irony—When He is in control, I am in control. There is no need to be frantic or anxious. My spirit discerns better through the day. His assignment for me could be to give a word of comfort to a person in the office elevator who is distraught. One day, it was to a person whose car was broken down on the road. I just yelled out the window, "Is there something I can do to help you? Can I call someone?" It seems simple, but that's the everyday business of Christianity.

When God is in control, I am more in tune with the needs of my business. I can hear more clearly the cautionary counsel of the Holy Spirit, whispering, *Move slowly on this deal. This business partnership is not a good fit.*

Business Failure

My worst business failure or misstep occurred when I acted too hasty and failed to seek proper counsel from God and other trusted advisers. The venture place was Omaha, Nebraska. A group of

THE CHICK in CHARGE

business men came to Atlanta looking to recruit African-American business to Nebraska. My first question was, *where on earth is Omaha?* Omaha was the last place on my radar to expand our security firm. But I was so intrigued.

In fact, I was so eager to grow into other states I broke protocol. Not only did I not seek God's counsel, I did not follow my company's business formula. Neither did I talk to anybody about my plan to branch out. It was a hurried and isolated decision I anxiously made. I could have saved myself a lot of trouble and money had I just taken the sage advice spelled out in Philippians 4:6—"Be anxious for nothing, but in every situation (including business deals) pray about everything with thanksgiving, and present your request to God. I did not do this. Instead, I traveled to Omaha and accepted a security contract that was well below market value. The recruiters had assured me and the several other out-of-town business owners that we had the full backing of the mayor, as we were there to help grow the city. They offered us business space as part of the deal, and even the Chamber of Commerce was on board. Everything seemed very encouraging.

The day I signed the contract and officially opened the Omaha branch of ALL(n)1 Security was a big media event. News reporters hovered all over us, snapping pictures of me posing with the mayor and other public figures. The big story was that the mayor was working with minority businesses from across the country to expand Omaha's economy. But it soon became increasingly clear that the sweet talk promises of partnership and economic development might have been just that. And the contract I so foolishly signed left me hamstrung.

My team could not set up a quality professional organization that would mirror what we did in Atlanta. The low value also left us no room to hire a professional team or to send management from Atlanta to Omaha to get the operation going. To make matters worse, we failed to conduct enough study on wages in Omaha, which were higher than wages in Atlanta. Nebraska also had a very low unemployment rate. So we did not have a large pool of people from which to hire security guards. These are all factors that we would typically have looked at to determine our fit. But this time, I just plunged headlong and recklessly into the deal. The venture was a big flop. The company lost more than thirty thousand dollars after only two weeks.

Looking back, I later determined it was all a farce. The mayor was facing a recall election, and in my judgment, the push to recruit minority businesses to town might have been a PR stunt to create good photo ops for the mayor. After he beat the recall he would no longer take my calls.

Harsh Lesson Learned

The moment you get off course, get anxious, and don't follow your own path you risk major failure. Very seldom do I share my "Omaha disaster" story. Perhaps I am still embarrassed. Most people who are acquainted with me know I am book smart, business savvy, and meticulous to a fault. I earnestly seek Godly direction. So few would believe Mary Parker could have failed so badly.

The thirty-thousand-dollar loss was one thing, but this debacle threatened to tarnish my integrity and ALL(n)1 Security's brand, which we worked fiercely to protect. Thankfully, I was able to write a letter and gracefully bow out of the contract after a few weeks. Our company faced threats from the city for breach of contract. But eventually, the matter was settled amicably.

The business failure was massive, and so was the lesson learned. I was reminded, in no uncertain terms, that my security and success are found in first seeking and following divine council. In all the times, I have trusted God on a business decision, and He's never steered me wrong.

The paramount lesson I learned is that businesses are blessed with breakthroughs when they make room to trust God and seek His direction. It's been my experience that when I violate this principle of trust and reliance, I hit lots of unnecessary roadblocks. Trying to run my multi-million dollar company without God's input would be financial suicide. However, when we operate in the will of God, Psalms 84:11 says, "No good thing will He withhold from those who do what is right." Business translation is to always do what is right for your customers, colleagues, and employees. It's a surefire strategy for success. So for Christian business owners who don't incorporate their core spiritual values into their boardroom dealings or the overall running of their company, they are not maximizing their potential profits. If they do, even if you hit a few road blocks along the way, their businesses will still flourish.

ALL(n)1 Security offers me a platform to deliver hope and spiritual security to those who are lost and need direction in life. I make it my business to share the word of God with them. Whether they believe or not, many of them will leave my presence with the understanding that Jesus truly is the CEO. Whether they believe He's the Son of God or prophet or, just another man, at least I know they received the introduction of who Jesus Christ really is. We are the instrument God uses to share his love on the streets, on the job, and at home with our families.

CHAPTER NINE
Help Without Hurting

I RECEIVED A DISTRESSING CALL EARLY ONE MORNING IN THE WINTER of 1987. My young cousin who lived in Chicago had been hit by a car. What made it even more heartbreaking was that his accident happened one year to the day his younger brother being killed in a car accident. Having two brothers die so tragically exactly a year apart was just too much grief for the family to bear. I was living in Michigan at the time, so some relatives and I frantically jumped in my car and made the two hour-long drive to Chicago in an hour, all the while tearfully praying to God to spare my cousin's life.

I got to the hospital to find his parents stricken with grief. As usual, it was my role to offer comfort as we all prayed for a miracle while anxiously awaiting word from the doctor. Sadly, it was not what we wanted to hear. I was sitting in a hospital phone booth with the door ajar, trying, without much success, to hold back the tears while consoling a weeping relative on the other end of the line. All of a sudden I felt a gentle touch on my shoulder, and heard a sweet angelic voice spoke.

"Don't cry. God's gonna fix it."

I turned around and came face to face with a frail little girl who could barely walk. It shook me for a moment because there she was consoling me when I probably should have been consoling her.

"Why are you crying?" she continued, expressing deep concern. "What happened?"

I was so shaken up and overcome with sorrow that it didn't register that I was about to pour out my soul to a child, and a noticeably sick child, at that.

"My nephew was hit by a car and he didn't make it," I sobbed, fumbling in my jacket pocket for a crumpled piece of tissue to dry my tears and blow my runny nose.

"Well, God is going to fix it," she tried to assure me with a sincere tone of compassion. "He doesn't always let everybody live. But He's gonna fix it, and you don't have to cry anymore."

I was stunned. I could not believe those insightful words were falling from the lips of a child. She was like an angel God had sent to comfort me. But this angel was a seven-year-old girl who was hooked to an oxygen tank and who slowly pushed an IV pole down the hospital hallway as we walked and talked.

"So why are you in the hospital?" I asked my new friend, who later introduced herself as Twanda.

"I am always in the hospital because I'm very sick. Actually, I could die any day."

"That's so sad!" I said softy, trying not to sound shocked by her matter-of-fact tone surrounding death.

"Yes, but God will fix it," Twanda repeated, just as confident this time as she had been when she initially said it.

Such huge faith in such a tiny body, I thought.

I learned that Twanda suffered from muscular dystrophy, and doctors had told her parents she had only a few more years to live. And here she was giving me encouragement, when by all appearances, it was I who needed to encourage her. Meeting my little angle in the hospital corridor that day proved to be a pivotal moment in my appreciation for giving. Twanda was proof-positive that the business of giving is not measured by just dollars and cents; it's also measured by the size of our giving heart. It's not just in tangible gifts but also in simple words of comfort offered at just the right time. It's a lesson I had to learn time and again.

THE BUSINESS OF GIVING BACK

Earlier on in business, I never saw a need I didn't try to fill. I would have probably argued with Jesus himself, who once said, "The poor you'll always have with you." At one point, my zeal to help the less fortunate became so misguided that it worried my brother Rick. Afraid I'd give away everything I owned and go broke, he stepped in and took control of my personal finances in an effort to protect me from myself.

Willy-nilly is how I'd describe my giving, and naturally, it often caused unreasonable, even ridiculous financial expectations from friends, some family members, even strangers. It seems the word was out—whatever the need just call Mary. *Someone in prison? Call Mary to bail them out. Your child needs money for college tuition? Call Mary. Someone's family member dies with no insurance, surely Mary will help us pay for the funeral.*

The requests for help were so relentless at times that I wasn't sure if I was empowering or just enabling people. Then, I learned the hard way that, sometimes, your giving only hurts you, not the person in need. A business colleague once got into a huge financial bind and needed thirty-five thousand dollars to make her payroll. Imagine her sigh of relief when I agreed to lend her the money and keep the company afloat. We agreed to a six-week repayment plan. This woman gave me five hundred dollars once and then refused to return my phone calls. She later lost the business, and, of course, I lost my money. I even once gave a friend several thousand dollars to pay her back mortgage to avoid foreclosure. It wasn't long before she eventually fell behind again and lost the house. Again, I was the big looser for tossing money to the wind.

One too many of these costly, good-intentioned bail-outs finally got me thinking—*Mary, you have got to build in some perimeters around your giving.* I needed to take charge! If not, I'd try to fix the financial problems of everyone who came to me with a need. This certainly can be one of the character flaws of a *Chick in Charge*—we often think we can fix everything for everybody. For too long it meant going into my pocket or writing a check to apply a band aid approach to someone's "emergency" or life crisis.

What a breakthrough when I finally accepted the fact that I'm not the answer to everybody's problems. With that matter properly settled in my head and heart, I felt more in control and less obligated to give at random. And gradually, I began to feel less guilty when I chose to *"just say no."*

Over the years, I've created an infrastructure for giving that is more selective and purpose-driven. It operates through my non-profit organization and is funded in part by corporate and individual sponsors as well as strategic partners who share my philanthropic vision. Gone are the days of being a haphazard giver. Great leaders and businesspersons can't be effective trying to help a hundred and one causes. Find a need that's near and dear to your heart. Develop a strategic plan just like you would for a business. Later, you can even form strategic alliances to help you expand your cause or charity work to reach more people in need. One of my first "selective giving" endeavors was born out of a need right under my nose at ALL(n)1 Security.

BOOK BAG CAMPAIGN

Imagine inviting three dozen rambunctious kids to your house for a Back-To-School party. This was the backdrop for my little get-together to give out book bags stuffed with school supplies to kids in need. I had noticed how a few of my mostly single mom employees struggled with purchasing school supplies every school year. It touched my heart, so I tactically chose to fill this need. The Back-To-School bash was held at my home in a wealthy, exclusive neighborhood because I wanted the children to see success. I wanted them to realize that entertainers, rappers and sports figures weren't the only successful African Americans. So, the objective was to expose the kids to a different face of success, one that they could touch, sit next to, play with and even call, Auntie Mary. Hopefully this expanded their idea of wealth and their own possibility thinking.

That first Back-to-School party was seven years ago and we gave away thirty seven book bags stuffed with school supplies. This year, we blessed nearly three hundred students with loaded book bags. One of the keys to expanding our reach was to get sponsors who shared our vision, invested in our proverbial sandbox and come out to play with us as we served the children. If you have a dream to give back by helping others, don't wait for the big bucks to roll in. Start where you are with what you have, like Twanda. All she had was a word of encouragement. It's never too small or soon to invest in the business of giving. As I mentioned earlier, as you grow, seek out strategic partners who share your cause and are committed to helping you change the world one good deed at a time.

SCHOLARSHIP DRIVE

Giving away book bags is good. But as a *Chick in Charge* who is always pushing the envelope, I had to ask myself, *how can I make my good better? How else can I raise other generations to excel in life?* The Mary Parker Foundation was created as an answer to these soul-searching questions. Its core purpose is to raise college scholarship funds to help deserving students with financial challenges. In just four years, the Mary Parker Foundation has awarded more than eighty thousand dollars in scholarships. To date, we are helping twenty-five students in seventeen colleges and universities.

But it's not enough to help the best and brightest kids excel. What about those who are left behind because they struggle to pass the ACT or the college admissions test? We have identified a way to help those young people prepare for these standardized test through a five-week training program. Statistics show that students who go through such training can increase their ACT scores dramatically. This means they'll be better qualified for MPF scholarships and to get into better schools. Better schools mean a better quality of education, which eventually leads to better employees in the workforces, or better business owners. Everybody wins when we invest in our children and our young people.

RESTRUCTURE PROGRAM

What about those young people who got in trouble with the law and are spending years wasting away in prison? Many were locked up on non-violent drug offenses and will be released with little to no viable job skills and a felony record that will likely haunt them to their grave. The Mary Parker Foundation has established a reentry training program to create relationships between the inmates and corporate America to prepare them to get jobs with companies once they are released. I believe we should be in the business of giving some of these inmates a chance to make it once they get out. The plight of these young men hit home when a nephew of mine went to prison for killing his girlfriend in a crime of passion. No, I do not condone his violent action. But him going through the "system" awakened me to some very ugly truths which are now being publically debated as the country grapples with warehousing African-American men, mainly as a result of the so-called "war on drugs." A recent news story in the Huffington Post, which sources the International Center for Prison Studies, almost shocked me to tears. Among other things, it quotes that, "There are more African American men incarcerated in the U.S. than the total prison populations in India, Argentina, Canada, Lebanon, Japan, Germany, Finland, Israel, and England combined." And just think, India alone has a population of 1.2 billion people. The fact that approximately 745,000 black men are locked up in jails and prisons across the country should trouble us all. This growing debate among some politicians, human rights advocates, and social activists centers on whether many non-violent drug offenders serving excessively long and harsh sentences should be released. If and when they are, how well will they assimilate into society? The foundation's reentry training program could provide a structure that gives inmates job-ready skills and potential employment on day one of their freedom. Just consider how giving that opportunity to an inmate could transform a life, a family, a community, and a nation.

Giving Abroad

Somehow I knew my purpose-driven efforts to serve and give back would one day go global. So, it was of little surprise when I visited Ghana in 2010, that one thing on the agenda was to find a need and fill it. I had traveled to the West African nation on a fact-finding trip to determine whether it was feasible to expand ALL(n)1 Security to that country. But what commanded much of my time was visiting an orphanage that I later adopted. The Osu House was home to about two hundred and fifty children, many frail and sickly. The policy at the orphanage prohibited strangers from holding the babies. But I couldn't resist, and they had to make an exception. It was painfully obvious that babies in the nursery were desperately hungry for the human touch. As I picked up one fragile little baby girl, she just wrapped her arms and legs around my body and settled in as though to say, "Ahh, I've been waiting so long to feel your warmth." The mother who ran the orphanage indicated that some of the children had been completely detached from their families—many were found on the side of the road and dropped off.

I had gone to the orphanage with nothing much to give that particular day, except a few lollipops and some Girl Scout cookies. I stood in the nursery weeping praying for the child in my arms, which was when her gentle touch took me back to a hospital in Chicago, to the gentle touch of a sweet, sick girl who whispered, "Don't cry, God's going to fix it." Twanda's giving spirit and her gentle reminder had never faded from my memory. But this time, God was going to use me to "fix it;" to improve life at the orphanage. I asked Ben, my business partner in Ghana, to take me to the nearest market, and there we stocked up on food and snacks to feed the children for a week. Before I left Ghana, which was several weeks later, I replenished the stock and made a commitment to send money to restock the food supply several times a year.

Are you about the business of giving? You don't have to take a trip to the other side of the world to give. Little Twanda taught me that you give what you have, however small, even if it's a touch of encouragement to a crying woman. Twanda died four years after we became friends, but not before I lavished her with gifts and threw her first-ever birthday party at Chucky Cheese, surrounded by playful kids, just way she wanted it. I also granted her make a wish foundation request to take a limousine ride to the beauty salon to get her nails and hair done. I suspect even in heaven my little angel is still about the business of giving someone a reason to be joyful.

CHAPTER TEN
Master the Trade and the Tricks

If you want something said, ask a man;
if you want something done, ask a woman.
Margaret Thatcher

THE OLD ADAGE SAYS THAT, "IF YOU WANT SOMETHING SAID ASK A man, if you want something done ask a woman." Those are the razor-sharp words of the irrepressible Margaret Thatcher. The first female Prime Minister of Great Britain was famously called the "Iron Lady." She had a determined spirit, a strong personality and delighted in sparing with rival colleagues who packed Britain's male-dominated Parliament. But I am sure even the iconic Margaret Thatcher would agree that to get some things done sometimes we women must be "as wise as a serpent and harmless as a dove." A serpent is quick to learn. A dove is innocent and gentle. Gentleness is perhaps one of the most formidable tactical weapons in the arsenal of a *Chick in Charge* who works in a male-dominated industry. Think of gentleness as strength under control. It's not always wise to bark orders because you can. Sometimes a subtle, back door approach to get things done is just as effective, especially if the front door is being barred by men who are threatened or intimidated by a woman's perceived power.

That was the case in one incident where I worked in 1989.

The manufacturing company faced a theft problem, and as head of security, I had to identify our vulnerability points and figure out who was involved in stealing company equipment.

"One thing's for sure, this is an inside job," I confided to a colleague who director of security at another manufacturing facility.

"How do you know?" he asked.

"Well, they know they can't get out of the plant with the equipment so they toss them over the fence in back of the plant," I explained. "Then they come back later to retrieve them. That's brazen."

I suspected someone in management had to be involved, because the stolen goods were not just production line products. Some are high value equipment that we kept under lock and key.

"Who are all the people who have a grand master key to the plant?" my business colleague inquired.

"I'm not sure," I admitted, as a cloud of worry rolled over my countenance.

My initial investigation had revealed that an alarming number of people had been issued grand master keys, which gave them full access to sensitive areas any time of the day or night. Most were supervisors and foremen who had been with the plant for years. Their grand master key was a symbol of power, access, and seniority privilege. But for the thief or thieves, it also opened a door to a crime that was costing the company tens of thousands of dollars.

"Tell your boss you've got to confiscate those keys," my colleague strongly insisted. "Change the locks on all the exterior doors and to the high-risk areas. Lock everybody out who doesn't need to be there. Then, retrieve those grand master keys."

I had sought out my colleague's advice, and knew it was sound. But I also knew my boss wouldn't look kindly on me swiping keys from his management staff. It would give me too much authority over a bunch of middle-age men who weren't about to take orders from a young black chick. I could just hear my boss' objection.

"Mary, some of these workers have had their grandmaster key for twenty years, and now you want to tell them to relinquish that key? They will see that as relinquishing their power to you."

So, what was I to do? Instead of me introducing the conversation to my boss directly, I devised a strategic back-door approach—invite my white male colleague to my plant for lunch and get my boss to join us. I did just that. While at lunch, I initiated a conversation about security treats and had my colleague share how his plant attacked internal theft via limiting grand master key access. Before long, my boss was sold on the idea of confiscating the keys, because it came from a source he was comfortable with—another man, with perceived credibility. The lesson here is if you can't beat them, sometimes just gently work around them. With my boss issuing the edict, and not me directly, we managed to implement an access control strategy that eliminated that theft problem.

THE BOARD ROOM MISSION

Back-dooring to get things done is just one of the "tricks of the trade" I have used in business. Another is choosing to sit on corporate boards with a definite mission in mind. My only child, Chana, might get offended, but I've always wanted a son as well. You might say that was my mission for joining the Atlanta Area Council of the Boy Scouts—to find a few "sons" to nurture and mentor. The real reason runs a bit deeper though. I had become aware of the many children in and around my church being reared by single parents. What was even more troubling was the alarming number of African-American boys going to prison. In this instance, we have men locked in prison and single moms too busy working to put food on the table to manage their wayward young sons. That was a recipe for a life or crime on the streets, if not careful. I strongly felt it was an urgent matter. I felt, as a community, we needed to move fast to save at-risk boys. And the best way for me to an impact their lives was to get involved in an organization that supported boys. This was the Boy Scouts. It offered a way for me to better understand boys and serve them at the same time. By strategically serving on the council, I was able to help establish two Boy Scout troops, including troop 1558 at my church. My position also gave me inside knowledge. So when I discovered that many of our scouts had never been outside their immediate community, I got them involved and a part of various out-of-town camps and other programs. I also leveraged my clout on the council to get uniforms for my troops because they couldn't afford them. Plus, we provided training for members of the community so they could get involved and assist the scout leader and den master. This is the power of joining a board with a mission in mind. It can change lives.

Securing a board seat is not always a purely philanthropic endeavor. There is nothing wrong with you asking yourself, *what's in it for my business?* When I sat on The Greater Women's Business Council the objective was to serve the council as well as get opportunities to grow ALL(n)1. The experience exposed me to more diverse companies and potential clients.

GWBC put me in front of Corporate America and gave me access to businesses I needed to market to. This type of promotional advertising was priceless. The trick is to be very intentional in accepting board positions. Be sure they align with a cause dear to you socially or professionally. Then learn to leverage your position and your relationships with fellow board members for a greater good.

THE FEMININE TOUCH

Male-dominated corporate boards are seeking women to serve as members for particular reasons, and it's certainly not to look like or act like a man. It's to bring our unique value to the table. Gone are the days (hopefully) when we females feel a pull to just fit in with their male counterparts. Remember the era of the dark "power suit" designed to disguise our femininity in the workplace? Those boxy Velcro shoulder pads that made us look more "businesslike" was all the fashion rave during the 1980s. Well, it turns out our unique feminine quality *was* our power! So here's a trick of the trade—if you really want to make your mark and stand out in business, don't ever leave your feminine qualities at the door when you step into a boardroom or business environment. Carry the presence of being a woman in with you, along with your expertise.

What is generally unique to women is our ability to view business through the lens of sensitivity. Our keen instinct and discerning spirit allow us to more readily balance hard facts and figures with heartfelt compassion. No one wants to run a business or a board meeting on emotion. But some experts believe emotional intelligence or EQ, might matter just as much if not more than one's IQ in attaining success in life and business. It is the emotional side of us that evokes feelings. And it's feelings that connect our hearts, builds trust, and creates bonds. This is how relationships are formed, whether with friends, families, colleagues or business clients. Perhaps women tap into their EQ more often than men because we are more maternal by nature.

I must admit though, trying to survive in a male-dominated industry hardened me emotionally earlier on. I can't say I was more compassionate than any other male-run company. I was in the trenches with them, fighting for my positions, for respect in the industry. I fought to be looked upon as equal, to be paid equal wages for the same work I did as my male colleagues. So even when I climbed to the top, I still had that fight to survive mentality. It was some time after building up ALL(n)1 Security that I came up for air and took careful note of my employees. I noticed that my past struggles were their present struggles. I, too, was a young single mom who worked different shifts and struggled with child care. And now I was in a position to show compassion and ease some of their hardship. So when a staff member's child got out of school before she got off work, the company's response to her dilemma was not, *Tough luck, it's your problem, deal with it.* We arranged for her to leave work, pick up her child from school every day and keep her at the office until the mother was schedule to clock out. When one of our security guard's wife had a baby, someone had to run his household which included several school age kids needing constant care. So we adjusted dad's shift to give him three to four weeks of paternity leave.

Eventually, we looked at re-designing the work shifts to better accommodate the varying family needs of all our employees. Instead of everybody working the same shift, we offered flexible schedules to allow employees to meet the changing demands of their family and other at-home needs. In the end, doing so helps to stabilize the family and make parents and children happier.

What's the payoff for me? When workers know you care they reciprocate by being more loyal and committed employees. So another trick of the trade is to take good care of your employees, and they'll take good care of you.

NETWORKING NONSENSE

Atlanta boasts the busiest international airport in the world. What might be even busier is the bevy of networking events that draw of entrepreneurs and business owners to mix and mingle around the clock. If your business is established and has a level of clout, expect a steady flow of invitations to exclusive networking parties. You can attend a conference luncheon, dinner or business panel discussion every day of the week.

I tried to keep up with this insanity for three years. I thought I was developing important business relationships. But that's not what networking is all about. What I was actually doing was socializing for three years. I stopped this nonsense once I clearly understood the strategy of effective networking, especially on a corporate level. The trick is to first analyze your purpose and identify a clear benefit for going to these events. If you can't, stay home and don't waste your time. Many of the companies that invited me to sit at their table understood the power of proper networking. I was the go-to- girl for their diversity and minority inclusion platform.

They would wisely and strategically utilize ALL(n)1, as a female-minority owned company to make a favorable impression at these events. And I would gladly oblige. I'd attend a high-profile luncheon at a big name company. Then I'd show up at dinner to press the flesh and network at another prominent corporate function across town. Next, I'd serve on a panel at a big business bash put on by another corporate giant.

Now, one would think my hobnobbing, networking and making countless appearances would lead to some potential new clients for ALL(n)1 Security. On the contrary, I realized I wasn't asking for the business. All I was doing was going out having chicken dinners, heavy hor d'oeuvres, and wilted garden salads on my dime. So I devised a strategy to take charge and become an important player. I needed to brand my company and become a sponsor at these top events. So, I became more selective with the events I chose to attend, and I invested the funds to get my company name prominently positioned on the main stage as a sponsor. And before I stepped out the door of my house, I had already determined, *what's in it for me.* I had investigated the big players expected at the event whom I needed to know, and established who needed to know me and what my company had to offer. And that's how I established my networking strategy that eliminated ninety percent of the nonsense socializing.

LET YOUR RELATIONSHIPS SELL YOU

As a business owner, it's not enough for people to know who you are. You must build relationships that also allow others to know what product or service you sell, who you sell to, and who is buying. In relationships, people get to know, like, and trust you. Once that's established, they'll be more inclined to recommend your business to their friends and colleagues. Just imagine, while you're home sleeping your friends are still going to those chicken dinners, and they're talking about *you.*

The conversation between a stranger and someone who has come to know and love Mary Parker and ALL(n)1 Security might unfold along these lines:

Concert Manager: "Yeah, my crew is new in town, just arrived from Los Angeles to plan a big concert for Jay Z's North American tour." First stop HOT-Lanta!

Local Businessman: "Oh, that's exciting! Atlanta is the Black Mecca of the South. So you know we are always ready to 'get down with it.' Anything I can do to help?"

Concert Manager: "Well, I'm looking for some serious security detail for the event. Got any suggestions?"

Local Businessman: "Oh yeah, I'd highly recommend ALL(n)1 Security. They do lots of special events including big concerts. They even offer executive celebrity protection. Plus, the Atlanta International Airport has been using their security surveillance services for the last six years."

Concert Manager: "Wow! That says a lot! Thanks. I'll check them out."

So that's what relationship building can do for your business. It can have people marketing and promoting your business anywhere, anytime, free of charge.

CHAPTER ELEVEN

The Student is Now the Teacher

*Today knowledge has power. It controls access to
opportunity and advancement.*
Peter Drucker

WHO WOULDN'T WANT TO GO TO WORK EVERY DAY AT A BUSINESS YOU created, to a job that you love and get paid a handsome salary to have fun? That's where I am in my life right now.

What's more, I get to lead others in finding their way to success in business. And this *Chick In Charge* wants to make sure you don't waste as much time or money, and make as many mistakes, as I did along the way.

My business-to-business mentor program called **"FACS"** is an acronym that stands for <u>**FOCUS**</u> <u>**ANALYZE**</u> <u>**COMMIT**</u> <u>**STRATEGY**</u>. These are four pivotal business principles that changed my life. I have used them to radically shift my business practice and increase my company's growth exponentially. FACS was birthed from this desire to transfer my knowledge to small businesses and start-up companies. The structure of FACS is also built on the lessons learned from my two decades of running multi-million dollar firms and ultimately thriving in male-dominated industries. Every year, I get the privilege to share my resources and knowledge with a new generation of eager entrepreneurs. I believe God trusted me with "the ability to get wealth" because He knew I would generously share with others and work to build them up.

Seeking the FACS of Business

Yes, indeed, I made countless mistakes as a new business owner. Even as ALL(n)1 Security grew and the world looked in with curiosity when the news media praised us as a model security firm, we were still tripping from internal missteps. But since failure is not encoded anywhere in my DNA, I have always been solution-driven. Sometimes, my mind flashes back to Uncle T's whisky distillation business. From that childhood experience I am constantly reminded that everything is a process. It took me years of trial and error to find the proverbial secret sauce to get the FACS myself. It took a determined search for answers to self-improve and fine tune my business. It meant being nosey enough to hunt down the hidden "tricks of the trade." Along the way, I discovered why certain doors of opportunities are shut tight to those naive enough to believe in business fair play, especially if your business involves government contracts. I learned it took bucking "the good ole' boy" system. It took being bold enough to challenge the status quo and defy the "business as usual" mentality. Getting the FACS meant being wise enough to attach myself to great and generous mentors. It meant heeding their sage advice forged from years of experience. And it demanded thousands of dollars of my hard-earned money to invest in continuing education and advanced industry training.

The FACS mentorship program distils the wealth of knowledge I gathered on my quest to develop a strong and sustaining business that secured my desired standard of living as well as my legacy. Each year, I hand pick a select group of entrepreneurs to experience the twelve month mentorship intensive. They come ready to take the bull by the horns, break through self-imposed barriers and learn insider strategies from the experts on how to accelerate business growth.

Many small business owners are CEOs wearing multiple hats. They wear themselves out to the point of exhaustion working sixteen-hour work days, as I did. The FACS program teaches mentees to put in place systems and processes that allow them to be more stable, efficient, and profitable.

FOCUS

When I started my first security company I only knew how to conduct the technical aspect of security, how to put on a security guard uniform and go out as "officer friendly" in whatever environment we worked. But I got stuck operating as an employee not an employer.

You may have heard the term, "Keep the main thing the main thing." Well, I was not focused on the main thing. When a new business owner falls into survival mode, they operates as a "chief cook and bottle washer" for too long, and he or she can quickly lose sight of the main thing—the business objective. I had to refocus on what I was selling, to whom I was selling it, when my customers bought it, and how much they were willing to pay for it. FACS mentees are taught how to focus on clearly defining their product or services, identifying their ideal clients, and building a team of business experts to help build and expand the enterprise.

ANALYZE

The "A" in FACS is analyze. Typically, I don't enter into any situation without first doing a SWOT analysis. It is crucial for any serious business owner to step back and determine their strengths, weaknesses, opportunities, and threats, or SWOT.

What natural abilities or academic skill sets do you or your team members already possess? What are you areas of needed growth? Identify opportunities of business possibilities and determine the threats that can impede your success. Conducting such a thorough analysis can help a business build a solid foundation. It also helps catch and correct internal threats that can, like hungry termites, secretly chew away at the structure of your house.

COMMITMENT

Before launching a business, decide your level of commitment. Whether your business requires wearing a security guard uniform, writing press releases, teaching people to speak, or preaching inside of your church, you must be committed if it is to succeed. Commitment is like the glue that keeps your business dream together when things appear to be falling apart.

Have you ever heard the story of the chicken and the pig? Well, it goes something like this:

Two guys sit down to have breakfast of eggs and bacon, and they engage in brief conversation.

"So, based on what's on our plate, what's the difference between the chicken and the pig?

"I don't know. What's the difference?" The other guy answered, a bit puzzled.

Displaying a mile-wide grin on his face, the first guy answered, "The chicken contributed, but the pig was committed. He gave it all up."

Here's the analogy explained. While it took little effort for the chicken to contribute an egg toward the meal, the pig's commitment showed that he had to die for the bacon to be produced. Likewise, in business, it takes dying to fear, outside criticism, self-doubt, and a host of other obstacles that will challenge our commitment to success. If you are not "sold out" for your own success, you won't be steadfast when your business hits the inevitable bumps in the road. Commitment is key to weathering the storms in business.

I've hit lots of pitfalls, suffered much pain, wasted a lot of money, and only God knows how much time because of my lack of commitment. Everybody needs the FACS to avoid repeating my mistakes.

READY TO BE THE BOSS?

Many people are just plain tired of their 9-to-5 jobs and feel they can do better being their own boss. According to the Small Business

Association, about 627,000 new businesses open each year in the U.S., but about 595,000 close each year as well. Many of these new start-ups are entrepreneurs who have worked for years in Corporate America where the glass ceiling has shattered their American dream, or they are just plain tired of clocking in and out on the 9-to-5.

Years of corporate layoffs and downsizing have infused fear in the job market and drastically changed the business landscape. Back in my days at GM, unions ruled the land. Even though I was never a union member due to my status as GM supervisor, I witnessed unions as strong protectors of worker's rights and wages. Union membership meant job security and a nice pension after thirty years at the local plant. But those glory days are in the past, as the strong arm of union has been greatly diminished over the years. Now, seasoned employees are forced to compete with a younger generation of workers who know less operationally but are increasingly more tech savvy. Some companies require existing employees to retrain, not just to stay abreast of swift changes being triggered by new technology. They are being pushed to multi-task and take on more duties and responsibilities, often with little to no pay increase. It's no wonder so many people are burned out and discouraged. It's no wonder so many are attracted to starting their own businesses.

You're the company's top insurance saleswoman seven years running and making the owner rich. Without you, the business would fall apart. Why settle for making sixty-five thousand dollars a year when you've got visions of making millions on your own? Why not reinvent yourself? Take your valuable skills and start an insurance consulting firm? That's the conversation "Jackie" had with herself many times. Finally, she decided to take the plunge and start her own business. In the first year, she struggles to get clients and stay afloat. By year three she is heavily in debt and very disillusioned. She struggles even more, and by year five, she files for bankruptcy and goes looking for another corporate job. Jackie represents tens of thousands of people who "got weary in well doing" as new entrepreneurs. They lacked the FACS of starting and running a successful new business.

STRATEGY

The last FACS principle is Strategy, and it's way more than having a business plan in your head or scribbled on a paper napkin. Strategy is your plan of action that spells out in copious details every step needed to execute your business. Strategy is the big "how" in the FACS equation. Developing a process to get to your desired results could be through people, processes, systems, investing, growing your business to scale. It could also mean branching into other areas and adding more services.

Our FACS business mentees spend time with business experts sharpening their Focus, their Analysis, their Commitment and their Strategy. At the end of the year-long training, they produce tangible evidence of implementation.

So, the FACS are that you've got to have crystal clear objectives and clear goals. Analyze or assess where you are in your business today. Raise your level of commitment and self-accountability. Develop strategies to accomplish those missions. Utilize these four phases and watch how well your business will begin to develop.

During the FACS course, participants will have measurable results they can take back to their places of business. They can use the same system taught to analyze and measure potential weaknesses and possible growth areas in their companies.

PREPPING COLLEGE STUDENTS

More than 1.4 million students graduate every year with a bachelor's degree from a four-year college or university somewhere in the U.S. Most have learned what it takes to get a J-O-B not so much how to become an entrepreneur. Astute business professors can give information on starting and running a successful business. But unless they have actually run their own business the lesson is just theory. Well, what if colleges spent a lot more time creating entrepreneurs than just churning out people with degrees who oftentimes aren't able to finds jobs? The Mary Parker Foundation is now partnering with colleges and universities to incorporate FACS in their curriculum. We are also working to create an entrepreneurial training program for middle and high school students. The earlier they get the FACS the sooner our young people can start thinking like serious business owners and deliberately begin shaping their future success.

CHAPTER TWELVE

Leaving a Legacy

Outlive your life!
Max Lucado

R EFLECTING ON A THIRTY YEAR CAREER CAN BE A DAUNTING TASK, especially if the journey was an aimless path without much direction, or paved with regrets over missed opportunities. Not so for me. I look back on my "long and winding road" with joy because, as a *Chick in Charge,* I seized just about every business opportunity that came my way. Where opportunities did not exist, I created them. Where they were blocked I fought to blast right through them or finessed to work around them. God has used me to break boundaries in the automotive and security industries, which are two of the most challenging career fields for women. I take great pride in knowing that my company, ALL(n)1 Security, is a thriving, multi-million dollar enterprise that provides a source of income for more than three hundred employees and their families. The security firm has enjoyed triple-digit growth under my leadership, and we have never once operated in the red. What's more important, service satisfaction has consistently ranked exceptionally high among our valued clients nationwide.

A wise soul once said, "The impossible is something that nobody can do until somebody does it." Some people said much of my business accomplishments couldn't be done, but they were proven wrong. I was both curious and courageous enough to try, just like that nosey child in Horse Pen who kept "getting in grown folks' business." Curiosity and courage have served me well in building an enterprise and establishing a wealth legacy for my entire family.

How do you pull away from a baby that you birthed and have nurtured, guided and watched grow into something great? You do it gradually. I started my succession plan for ALL(n)1 Security in 2014 by relinquishing the title of president to my brother and business partner. Serving solely as company CEO has freed me up from the day-to-day operation. That gives me more time to build my legacy through the Mary Parker Foundation, which creates, identifies and supports local, national and global causes I care about. I also am freer to travel throughout the country and speak to Criminal Justice students, mentor women and minorities interested in the security profession, which is a passion.

More time also allows me the chance to pursue other business ventures, like starting ABD Contracting LLC, in 2013. It's a full service concrete and asphalt paving company which offers services including installation, coding and maintenance. We operate in Alabama and Georgia. In starting company, I took a from Roy Robert's business playbook. Roberts is a friend and mentor who once shared with me the difference between an entrepreneur and an enterpriser. During one of our many conversations we had when we worked together at General Motors, explained to me the crucial difference between the two.

"Mary, remember this. An entrepreneur starts a company and that's all they will do. An enterpriser starts multiple companies that spring from their main business brand. They also buy or partner with companies that offer major financial investment opportunities."

Roy later rose to become the highest-ranking African American in the automobile industry. After retiring from GM, he started several hugely successful businesses. Roy once told Forbes Magazine what drove him to succeed was a simple philosophy his father drilled into his head— "Work to be better not equal." His personal counsel helped shape my own drive for success well beyond our time together at GM. Roy would be pleased to know that along with ABD Contracting, my next enterprising frontier is investing in a health-based franchise, yet another brick in building my wealth legacy.

Legacy building has also meant shifting some personal expectations and shutting some painful doors. First, the Expectations: I expected my daughter, Chana, to succeed me at the helm of ALL(n)1. It would have been a natural process for her to inherit the business I worked so hard to build from scratch. In all fairness to our children, though, we must allow them the opportunity and freedom to explore career paths that stir their passion, plus bring them joy and satisfaction. So even though my brother Rick is quite capable of running the company, initially, I had envisioned ALL(n)1 as a three-generational female-owned security business—to be headed by me, my daughter, then my granddaughter. Three consecutive *Chicks In Charge*. Now, my nephew, Clarence Powell, is getting hands on training as another leader in the organization. Having him and Rick in place ensures that ALL(n)1 will remain in the family and part of my legacy. As I set myself up to retire, I've spent years transferring knowledge to my core team. With Rick's innovative push to integrate changing technology to serve our clients and expand the business to new frontiers, I am confident the company will remain a viable leader in the security industry for generations to come.

However, legacy is not always positive. Some people have left a legacy of pain, misunderstanding and family dysfunction. As to shutting painful doors I mentioned earlier, my long unresolved friction with my father had left a legacy of deep, hurtful feelings. As you know even as a child, I never felt as though my father loved me. Even years after I left the plantation in Horse Pen, we only spoke on the few occasions when I went back to visit. Miraculously, two weeks before his death, I talked with him when he called Aunt Mae's house in Michigan.

"Helen, I don't know the last time I heard your voice," my dad said with cheerfulness in his voice, which was something unfamiliar to me. At the same time, however, it destroyed any doubt I had that he truly wanted to talk to me. As a matter of fact, we were pretty giddy throughout our conversation, which was spent on updating each other on what was going on in our respective lives.

For the first time, I truly realized that my dad really did love me. The lingering legacy of childhood hurt was about to be healed, I thought. I made hurried plans for my father to leave Horse Pen as soon as possible and come live with me, while he and my mom sorted things out. She had had enough of the sharecropping misery of the south and had finally left for Michigan with the five minor children three months earlier.

I spent the next couple of days after our conversation planning for our rushed reunion, imagining him stepping off the same train I took out of Mississippi so many years before. But unfortunately, the reunion would not take place. My dad died just a few days after our phone conversation, and so did my hope of reconciliation. I felt empty, disillusioned, and angrily questioned God. My dad was only forty-one years old. I guess years of drowning himself in Uncle T's moonshine liquor had taken its toll.

For seven years I refused to accept or grieve my dad's death, and I was dogged by the haunting question, what if? What if we had reunited? Would he have shed light on why it seemed he disliked me so as a child? Would it have provided some insight on why he targeted me for beatings and treated me as the black sheep of the family? After a while the questions or answers didn't matter. I had just wanted to see my dad.

Well, eventually God revealed to me the purpose of that last conversation with my father. He allowed it for dad to obtain a peace with me in order to die in peace. For me, God allowed me to accept the love from my dad that I never knew. One day, while visiting his gravesite I told him that I accepted his love and that I believe he would be proud of me. The experience was a refreshing release. In my heart, it rewrote a of my father's legacy concerning me. I had inherited the great satisfaction of now knowing that L.A. Robinson did indeed love his second daughter, Helen, just like Gran had assured me so many years ago. And that was priceless to me.

The funny thing about life is that no matter how old, how powerful, or even how wealthy a person gets, what really matters is the simple things that satisfy the yearning of our heart, which is to be loved, acknowledged, and affirmed. And we tend to seek affirmation from our parents, so on a separate note, it bothered me that no matter what I accomplished, my mother never seemed to praise me.

"I am proud of all my children," she would famously say.

But what I heard was, "You are not important, Helen, no matter how many or how great your accomplishments, it's not important enough to single you out."

Of course that's certainly not what my mother thought. But perhaps experiences from her past related to her relationship with her siblings caused hard feelings. And it made her decide never to treat any of her nine children any more special than the other. It took my sister Bobbie to bring the matter to mom's attention the night I received the prestigious Trumpet Awards in 2012.

As I recall, I was wound up tight like a ball of nerves, anxiously bouncing from one corner of the room to another. Bobbie was about to pray to calm me down when I said,

"It would mean so much to me if mom would just tell me she was proud of me,"

`Bobbie thought for a moment, then dashed downstairs where our mother was waiting. "I know you've always been adamant about not singling any of us out as it relates to our success, and how proud you are of us, but today is different," Bobbie said to my mother, her way of bringing the subject to the forefront.

My mother sat silently and listened as Bobbie continued.

"This award Helen is being honored with is much more than any of us will ever get in our lifetime. So I think it would be most appropriate if you went upstairs and talked with Helen, tell her how proud you are of just her."

"Of course, Bobbie," my mother replied, seeming a bit taken aback with concern. "I have no problem doing that."

What happened next was one of the most beautiful and uplifting moments of my life. My mother came up to my prayer room, took me in her arms and told me just how much she loved and was proud of me. I fell into her embrace like a wilted flower soaking up her refreshing words of comfort.

"If I ever made you feel that I was not proud of you, I apologize," my mother assured me, still cradling me in her arms. And then she prayed a prayer that instantly brought strength to my weak limbs. I felt so affirmed that moment that it didn't matter what anybody said going forward, because my mother told me she was proud of *me*.

That night actor Blair Underwood presented me with the Trumpet Award for Business. Even being on stage with the Hollywood heartthrob could not trump the delightful feeling of affirmation from mom. I must admit, though, it came close.

Perhaps I needed affirmation from both my parents because out of all my siblings, I spent the least amount of time with them, since I lived mostly with my grandmother. The chance to reconcile my feelings with both parents helped shift the legacy of our relationships.

In 2015, I went back to visit my old stomping ground in Horse Pen, just outside Grenada, Mississippi. I stopped by Billy Frank's house, as I sometimes do when I visit the area. He moved back years ago to the farming town. It was Billy Frank's "going off to college to get an education" that sparked my early determination to leave Horse Pen and don't come back until I was educated and could run the sharecropping plantation. I got the education alright, but found the world to be much bigger than Horse Pen, with way more opportunities to own and "run things" somewhere else.

To get to my "gated community" I drove by acres of cotton fields ripe for the picking, but the laborers were few. All that's left of the old days of sharecropping are memories of the sad legacy of a time gone by. I finally got to the old homestead to find a wide open field with a few dilapidated old houses dotting the bare pasture. The only residents were a herd of cattle who slowly gathered around me as though I had come to set them free, as all my relatives had been.

Several batches of wild yellow daffodils marked the grassy spot where my parents' two-room rental house once stood. I tried to retrace the steps my little feet would have made from there to grandmother's house where I spent so much of my childhood days. As if it were only yesterday, I heard Gran's sweet voice calling me.

"Helen, it's time to get to work little girl. Come wash out those mason jars for Gran. We got some canning to do."

For decades grandmother had refused to leave Mississippi, until her son, and my father died. Her daughters then took her to Chicago and later put her in a nursing home, which distressed me greatly. So one day I visited the facility and signed her out, and took her to live with me. Some relatives claim I kidnapped Grandma, and suggested notifying my aunts, letting them know Gran was in Michigan with me. She was the original *Chick in Charge* who left me a legacy of hard work, courage, commitment and a love for running a business and owning your own. And that's the legacy I now leave for everyone touch through ALL(n)1 and The Mary Parker Foundation that's transforming lives, and making the world better.

Grandmother is in heaven now. But I imagined having one more conversation with her on the very plot where I sometimes sat as a child to take in "grown folks business."

"Gran, you know my success is your success. It's all rooted in God and in your early guidance. You'd be so happy to know I've taken up your mantle not just in business, but to also to give back, and make sure no one is left behind."

"Baby," I could hear her say, "If any of them chilen's made it I knew it would be you. I am so proud of you."

"Thank you Gran. Because you were, I am ... a *Chick in Charge*."

Chick in Charge

A *Chick in Charge* doesn't wait for the tide to turn in her favor. She makes her own waves. She doesn't dance to the beat of a different drummer. She creates her own music and helps others to do the same.

Don't mistake her for a Diva. She is here on the planet to serve, not to be served. She's clear about her mission and stays in her lane. She focuses on the task at hand and does whatever it takes to get it done. She is misunderstood and mislabeled. Yet, critics don't disturb her. She is full of love and laughter. For, she makes it her business to be happy. She sips life from a full cup. The thought of lack or limit is not tolerated. She makes no apologies for following her dreams. And she makes no excuses for failing. She is quick to find her footing and try again. Weakness doesn't worry her. They are mere opportunities to develop strength.

Some say she's bossy and abrasive. Others say she's generous to a fault. From a distance, it's easy to focus on her flamboyance. Come closer, you'll find a woman rooted in faith and family. Her boldness and self-confidence come from a deep trust in God. She truly believes Him when he says:

"Seek and you shall find."
"In me all things are possible.
"Declare a thing and it shall be done."
"To whom much is given, much is required."
"You can do all things through Christ who strengthens you."

A *Chick in Charge* knows she is responsible to help change the world. And oftentimes, her no-nonsense approach offends. She finds no comfort in being a people-pleaser. Her joy stems from using her influence and resources to feed the needy, cloth the naked, and open blind eyes, whether physical, spiritual, or professional. What could be a higher, nobler charge?

Like this *Chick in Charge*, all of us are equipped with gifts and talents for the expressed purpose of serving humanity to the best of our ability.

Okay Chick, how will you now take charge to change the world?

BUSINESS RESOURCES & REFERENCE GUIDE

MARKETING

- Google+ – Google is a power house, this is no surprise. Originally launched as a search engine company in 1996, Google has continually added, updated and created new products that will ap-peal to it's1 billion unique visitors per month. Google.com

- HubSpot – HubSpot is an inbound marketing software plat-form that helps companies attract visi-tors, convert leads, and close customers. The software contains everything you need to do internet marketing. From blogging, to email and social - it's an all-in-one integrated solution. HubSpot.com

- Mashable – is a leading global media company that informs, inspires and entertains the digital generation. Mashable is redefining storytelling by documenting and shaping the digital revolution in a new voice, new formats and cutting-edge technologies. Mashable.com

RESOURCES

- Entrepreneur – This is a site that is loaded with helpful guides that will help your business to grow. Information you can find includes franchising, setting work schedules with teams, finding new ways to make money, and much more. Entrepreneur.com

- Flipboard – Your Personal Magazine with the world's best sources organized into thousands of topics, it's a single place to follow the stories and people that matter to you. FlipBoard.com

- Lifehacker – Part of the Gawker Media empire, but a bit on the tamer side than the regular stuff. You will find information here that is going to help to improve your life, as well as your business. Lifehacker.com

- SCORE – This site will give you loads of free advice from amazing mentors who have plenty of experience to share. You can even meet your mentors in person, as well as get free newsletters. Learn about a number of small business topics, from office security to mobile technologies and more. Score.org

- TechCrunch – TechCrunch is a leading technology media property, dedicated to obsessively pro-filing startups, reviewing new Internet products, and breaking tech news. TechCrunch.com

SUPPORT

- Small Business Administration – This is a government branch that helps entrepreneurs. You can use this site to get funding, find employees, and a whole lot more. SBA.gov

- Legal Zoom – LegalZoom is the nation's leading provider of personalized, online legal solutions and legal documents for small business owners and families. LegalZoom.com

- Shake – This is a new site that provides information on the legalities involved in operating your own small business. Use the mobile app to create contracts that can be signed immediately. The blog will explain the legal terminology used in your contracts. ShakeLaw.com

- Grow Smarta

NEWS IN BUSINESS

- CNBC Small Business – When it comes to business news, this is one of the most popular and well-known names in the industry. Articles are frequently updated, and you will find new infor-mation every time you visit. CNBC.com

- Businessweek – Find the latest business news, from economic trends to new mergers and more. This publi-cation offers a section just for small businesses, as well as plenty of other great infor-mation. BusinessWeek.com

- Fast Company – This is a business publication with a focus on creativity and innovation. Find any topic about small businesses, written uniquely. Stories can range from tips for marketing on social media to profiles and more, plus there are loads of great tips you can use. FastCompany.com

- Fortune – One of the changes you will notice about Fortune is the lack of ads. You no longer have to wade through ads to get to the information you really want, with topics on everything from small businesses to finance. Fortune.com

- Huffington Post Small Business – If you want business news in a hurry, this is the website to check out. Find short articles that anyone can read easily (not loaded with a bunch of jargon), and use this publication is a resource for your business. HuffingtonPost.com

- Minority Business Enterprise Magazine

MEMBERSHIP ORGANIZATIONS

- ASIS International

  www.asisonline.org

- International Organization of Black Security Executives

  www.IOBSE.org

- Vistage International

  www.vistage.com/international

- Women Business Enterprise National Council

  www.WBENC.org

- National Association of Women Business Owners

  www. NAWBO.org

- Women in Public Policy

  www.wipp.org

- National Minority Supplier Development Council

  www.NMSDC.org

- Atlanta Business League

  www.Atlantabusinessleague.org

- Local Business and Industry membership organizations available online.

About Mary H. Parker

When Mary H. Parker was a child, few people expected much from her. After all, she was a Mississippi born, black girl. And such children weren't always encouraged to complete high school, much less earn advanced degrees and develop a level of self- awareness that could propel them into positions of leadership. But Mary Parker did all of that, and more. She grew into a woman motivated to make a difference. It took some doing, her parents moved her out of Mississippi to Michigan to escape potential dangers and to improve her chance at a better life.

The move from Mississippi to Michigan gave Mary a glimpse at life's better options. She discovered her raw personal and professional abilities which she turned into skills through education, hard work and shrewd thinking. Mary wanted the finer things in life for herself and her family. And she knew that to earn them she had to think critically.

She made choices, though, that many people didn't understand. For example, she immersed herself into the field of criminal justice so she could start a security company. Many people may assume low-paid, poorly educated, hourly help when they think of a security and security guards. But Mary looked at the people who ran the industry. What she saw was a lavishly funded, Male-dominated, virtually all- white arena where she could excel. And she did.

Of course, Mary didn't make flawless decisions at every turn. She made human mistakes, which means she flunked a few life tests. But she pulled on her faith in God to pull her through.

Mary Parker's story contains a lot of facts readers won't expect. Learning about her journey to becoming *The Chick in Charge* provides almost everyone who picks up a copy, with a thought-provoking, entertaining read.

LOOK FOR THE CHICK *in* CHARGE ON SOCIAL MEDIA!

TWITTER • @thechickncharge

PERISCOPE • thechickncharge

INSTAGRAM • thechickncharge

FACEBOOK • www.facebook.com/mary.parker.58118774